Cure for the Common Church requires church leaders to step back and marry big picture with practical application. This immensely practical book will give you needed tools to lead a church through a revitalization journey.

—**Ed Stetzer**, president, LifeWay Research

Cure for the Common Church provides a much-needed practical guide to assist local church leaders in setting a path for renewal and growth. In plain language, it provides step-by-step instructions to lead strategic planning groups through complex issues. The approach is both comprehensive and instructive, providing a rich array of resources to facilitate self-examination and bring about significant changes without imposing a one-size-fits-all approach.

—**Eddie Gibbs**, senior professor, Fuller Theological Seminary

Need a little help diagnosing your church's spiritual malaise? The doctor is in. Dr. Bob Whitesel blends research and data with a remedial touch that feels achievable, simple, and wise in one stroke. Leaders and those simply interested in the health of their local churches would do well to pay attention to *Cure for the Common Church*. This isn't another book on church growth principles, but a prescription for spiritual vitality for congregations of every size.

—**Dave Workman**, author of *The Outward Focused Life*; senior pastor, Vineyard Community Church, Cincinnati, Ohio

What an insightful, problem-solving resource! Church leaders often get sidetracked by the symptoms of ill health and never identify the actual problem. This unique book clarifies the real issues and provides insights to help address them.

—**Charles Arn**, professor of outreach, Wesley Seminary, Marion, Indiana

CURE
FOR THE
COMMON CHURCH

God's Plan to Restore Church Health

Bob Whitesel

wesleyan
publishing
house

Indianapolis, Indiana

Copyright © 2012 by Bob Whitesel
Published by Wesleyan Publishing House
Indianapolis, Indiana 46250
Printed in the United States of America
ISBN: 978-0-89827-587-2

Library of Congress Cataloging-in-Publication Data

Whitesel, Bob.
  Cure for the common church : God's plan to restore church health / Bob Whitesel.
    p. cm.
  Includes bibliographical references (p.).
  ISBN 978-0-89827-587-2
  1. Church growth. 2. Church renewal. I. Title.
  BV652.25.W45 2012
  253--dc23
                                        2012024272

To Rebecca

CONTENTS

Additional resources and complete notes
are available online at www.wesleyan.org/wph/cureresources.

ACKNOWLEDGEMENTS |

This book would not have been possible without my church consultation clients who have yielded great insights over the past two decades. You have allowed me to travel along on your spiritual journey, observing innovations that led to renewal and growth. And I appreciate my seminary students who gave me ongoing feedback as together we fine-tuned these prescriptions. Their daily feedback coupled with my busy consultation schedule has helped me formulate cures that are relevant and effective. I am thankful for churches and people who, though desperate in the midst of calamity, saw a lesson for others and themselves. As Paul wrote to the Corinthians: "The trial exposed their true colors: They were incredibly happy, though desperately poor" (2 Cor. 8:2 MSG).

To the pioneers in the field of missional church leadership and growth, I owe an undying appreciation for the depths you have plumbed. Eddie Gibbs and Elmer Towns have not only been research colleagues, but personal mentors. Academic colleagues such as Richard Peace, Ryan Bolger, Scot McKnight, and Len Sweet have afforded my theories their scrutiny and insightful discussion. And to colleagues and close friends such as Gary McIntosh, Chip Arn, Dan Kimball, Kent Hunter, Tom Harper, Ken Schenck, Russ Gunsalus, Keith Drury, Colleen Derr, Lenny Luchetti, John Drury, and Wayne Schmidt, I owe a heartfelt thank you for your professional insights and boundless friendship.

I am even more thankful for the lovely family that God has given me, beginning with my college sweetheart and soul mate Rebecca. Our love has nurtured a new generation of wonderful lives that are touching others, including Breanna, Mark, Cate, Abbey, Kelly, Tory, Kai, Corrie, Dave, Capri, Ashley, and C. J. It would be impossible to balance my family, teaching, writing, and spiritual life without their unwavering prayers and love.

And finally and most of all I am thankful to my Lord Jesus, who daily teaches me more about his enormous love for the wholeness and health of his church: "Christ's love makes the church whole. His words evoke her beauty. Everything he does and says is designed to bring the best out of her, dressing her in dazzling white silk, radiant with holiness" (Eph. 5:26–27 MSG).

Bob Whitesel DMin, PhD
Professor of Missional Leadership
Wesley Seminary at Indiana Wesleyan University
www.BobWhitesel.com

QUICK-START GUIDE |

To help you find out which illnesses you have
and which chapters to read first.

WHO IS THIS BOOK WRITTEN FOR?

This book is primarily designed to help the average church
member understand how to renew and grow a church. This first
chapter is a Quick-Start Guide that will allow you to quickly identify
problems and then go directly to the chapters that address the cures
your church needs.

This book is also useful for pastors and denominational leaders.
Though church volunteer leaders can administer the cures
described here, pastors and denominational leaders will find that
this is the one place where all the major illnesses that impair
churches are diagnosed and their field-tested cures are presented.
These cures are based on twenty-plus years of church growth
consulting, ten books, and two earned doctorates from Fuller
Theological Seminary.

HOW DOES THE CURE WORK?

First use figure A (p. 13) to identify your church problems.
Adjacent to each problem is the chapter from this book that
addresses that problem. You do not need to read the entire book
if your problem is addressed in just a few chapters.

A true cure will only be effective if it is driven by church
members, because the average churchgoer will still be in a
church long after the pastor is gone. Thus, the most effective way
to get a church back on the road to long-term health is for these

churchgoers to identify the problem and administer the cure themselves.

There are four basic cures (each comprised of several prescriptions). Church members will form T.E.A.M. groups that investigate the prescriptions that are right for your church. There will be one to four T.E.A.M. groups based upon the severity of your problem. T.E.A.M. is an acronym for:

- Treatment: Each team will investigate one cure and suggest a treatment based on the prescriptions in this book.[1]
- Educate: Each team will educate the congregation and other T.E.A.M. groups about the church problem(s) and the cure(s).
- Action Plan: Each team will draft a plan for action.
  - ▶ Sometimes a T.E.A.M. will do the plan of action itself.
  - ▶ Other times a T.E.A.M. may delegate the plan of action to an appropriate group within the church and monitor its progress.
  - ▶ Each T.E.A.M.'s major focus will be to generate a workable action plan from the cures in this book.
- Measure Progress: Each T.E.A.M. will create four-month goals. At the end of four months, all T.E.A.M.s will come together and share their progress, holding one another accountable.

WHAT IS YOUR PROBLEM?

Use figure A to identify your problems and which chapters to read first.

Figure A: _Identifying Your Church Problems and Your Cures_				
	Chapters that address this problem[2]			
Church Problem[3]	2	4	6	8
Circle _both_ checkmarks in all rows that apply				
Congregation divided into factions	✓		✓	
Immorality in the church			✓	✓
Leaders have left unexpectedly	✓		✓	
Decline in attendance after a building program, relocation, or merger	✓	✓		
High pastoral turnover		✓	✓	
New ethnicities moving into the neighborhood	✓	✓		
Aging congregation	✓			✓
High turnover in attendees		✓	✓	
Newcomers usually don't stay longer than eighteen months		✓		✓
Few newcomers visit unless they are visiting the area or attendees	✓			✓
Part-time pastor		✓	✓	
Recently fired staff		✓	✓	
Church controlled by a small group of leaders or an extended family			✓	✓
Worship is dated and not reaching younger generations	✓			✓
Administrative boards are divided	✓		✓	
Pastoral staff makes most of the important church decisions		✓	✓	
Leaders and/or attendees have left to start a new church	✓	✓		
Leaders use their power for selfish goals	✓			✓
Church is focused mainly on its own needs	✓	✓		
Church facilities need expensive repairs		✓	✓	
Most of attendees have been Christians for many years	✓			✓
The church is too close-knit for its own good	✓	✓		
Church has a culture of dishonesty			✓	✓
Community residents are moving out of the area	✓	✓		
Church has its own way of doing things and new people don't easily adjust			✓	✓
Most of the congregation is living on a fixed income	✓	✓		
Church has suffered a public scandal in the last five years		✓		✓
Church has a poor reputation in the community	✓		✓	
Staff divided into factions			✓	✓
Income levels of attendees is declining	✓			✓
Church facility is hidden from much of the community		✓		✓
Cultural differences between churchgoers and non-churchgoers	✓	✓		
Church cannot pay its bills		✓	✓	
Church facilities are thwarting growth		✓		✓
Church attendees are not as passionate about God as they once were		✓	✓	
Church community outreaches have resulted in little attendance growth	✓			✓
Many attendees have limited knowledge about the Bible			✓	✓
Trouble getting people to volunteer			✓	✓
None of the above[4]	✓	✓	✓	✓
TOTAL (Add up in each column the total number of checkmarks you circled. The chapters with the most circled checkmarks contain the cures that should be addressed first.)				

What Is Your Cure?

Total the Number of Checkmarks You Circled in the Four Right Columns of Figure A. The columns with the most circled checkmarks should be the chapters with the most relevant cure for your situation.

Meet with Other Congregants. Share your results and decide as a group which chapters will be the most helpful for your situation.

If most of your checkmarks are in just one or two columns, you may find that you only need to read one or two cures. Other times, three chapters or all four chapters will need to be read.

If you do not have enough church leaders to form four teams, start by forming T.E.A.M. groups for the most relevant cures.

Ask Congregants to Participate in One of the T.E.A.M.s. Each congregant participates in only one team. Each T.E.A.M. will:

- Read the relevant **CURE** chapter.
- Meet at least once a month over the next four months to
  - ▶ T = Find appropriate **T**reatments,
  - ▶ E = **E**ducate the church about the best treatment,
  - ▶ A = Make an **A**ction plan, and
  - ▶ M = Decide how to **M**easure progress.
- Select
  - ▶ A convener who will arrange monthly meetings, chair the meetings, encourage attendance, and report progress.
  - ▶ A secretary who will announce meetings, secure meeting space and location, provide copies of actions plans and books, take meeting notes, and edit the plan of action.

All T.E.A.M.s Will:

- Join together every four months with all T.E.A.M.s to check progress and for accountability (until they all agree the cure is accomplished or sufficiently delegated).
- Join together once a year with all congregants to reexamine and revise their cures (see pp. 160–167 for details).

What Is the Purpose of Why and How Chapters?

Each cure is given two chapters:

- The why chapters explain why each cure is important. If you would like more information about the reasons behind each cure, then consult the why chapters. Others will consult the why chapters when they simply want more information.
- The how chapters explain how to administer the cure. If your church is in a crisis, you may want to skip the why chapters for now. This allows you to concentrate on the how chapters so a church can quickly get back on the road to renewal and growth.[5]

What Does the Magnifying Glass Symbol Represent?

Because this book is to the point and easy to read, additional information has been made available online at www.wesleyan.org/wph/cureresources. When you see a magnifying glass (like this example), it indicates that there are more insights in the online appendixes, which you can download and examine for more insights into each cure.

TAKE A **LOOK**

For More Information Read:
- An appendix will be cited here
- Another appendix may be cited here

WHY IS RENEWAL AND GROWTH SO IMPORTANT?

Why the Common Church Is So Widespread

Today the average or common church in North America averages around seventy-five attendees.[6] Over twenty years of consulting work has led me to believe that a church needs to average around 175 attendees for it to have the level of staff and ministries that most people have come to expect from churches today.

Less than a century ago, the church was the social hub of most communities, but today multiple social competitors have arisen. Some polls have suggested that only 40 percent of Americans go to church, but other researchers have found that people exaggerate how often they attend church and the actual number is about 18 percent.[7] Regardless of the percentage, the church in North America no longer enjoys the status of being the place to be on Sunday mornings. One author summarized, "The crisis, most simply put, is that the social function the churches once fulfilled in American life is gone."[8]

Add to this that churches are aging or embroiled in conflict, and you can see that the average or common church is unhealthy, either being too small, too divided, or too discouraged to grow.

Why Should Your Church Be an Uncommon Church?

There are thousands of churches making the switch from conflict, decline, and marginalization to renewal and growth.[9] They are bucking the trend and becoming uncommon churches in a world where the common church is marginalized at best, and dying at worst.

These chapters are the result of not only my years of church growth consulting, writing, and research on the cures for the common church, but they are also combined with the best insights from my fellow researchers.[10] It is my desire to put our best advice for renewal and growth into one book that will help average church leaders quickly get their church back on the path to growth!

God's Desire for an Uncommon Church

God, too, desires something more than the conflicted, ill, and marginalized church that is common today. Jesus stated in no uncertain terms that the church was to be the beacon of hope, the place of refuge, and the source of good news to a despondent and conflicted world. To remind us of God's wishes for his church, this chapter ends with a brief selection of Scriptures. It is toward helping the church overcome her poor health and return to growth and strength that these cures are aimed.

"The church grew. They were permeated with a deep sense of reverence for God. The Holy Spirit was with them, strengthening them. They prospered wonderfully" (Acts 9:31 MSG).

"The way God designed our bodies is a model for understanding our lives together as a church: every part dependent on every other part. . . . If one part hurts, every other part is involved in the hurt, and in the healing. If one part flourishes, every other part enters into the exuberance" (1 Cor. 12:25–26 MSG).

Paul wrote, "The focus of my letter wasn't on punishing the offender but on getting you to take responsibility for the health of the church" (2 Cor. 2:9 MSG).

There Is No Time to Waste!

Go back to figure A and find the most critical cures for the most pressing problems of your church. Then use T.E.A.M.s to begin to investigate, plan, and grow back into health. God has promised to help you (2 Cor. 4:7–11), because, after all, he wants an exceptionally uncommon church, too.

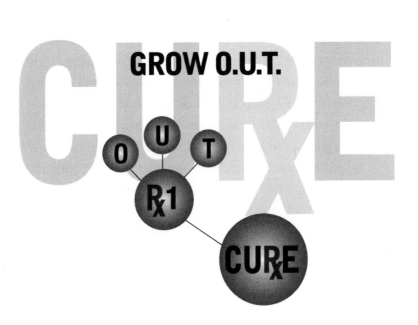

GROW O.U.T.

WHY GROW O.U.T.? | 1

"Yours may be a COMMON CHURCH if . . ."

(SELF-SCORING—Check all that apply)

☐ Your church has a long history in the community.

☐ Church volunteers stay longer in leadership positions than they want to.

☐ Your church sponsors events for the community but few community residents attend.

☐ Your church has a daycare and/or preschool but few of the parents attend your church.

☐ There is a lot of bickering and fighting in your church.

☐ Your church spends a lot of energy and money trying to have a better Sunday service.

☐ Your closest friends are also churchgoers.

☐ Most of your church volunteers live outside of the area in which the church is located.

☐ Few newcomers visit your church and those who do often stop attending within eighteen months.

☐ Most of your church attendees live outside the area in which the church is located.

☐ Your paid staff and volunteers spend most of their time focusing on church needs.

☐ Your church often argues about money, styles of music, or leadership decisions.

☐ You have an outreach committee or person with the responsibility of reaching out to others.

THE COMMON CHURCH IS OFTEN INGROWN

Slowly over time most churches grow primarily inward in their focus, rather than focusing outward to meet the needs of those outside the church.[1] The result of this inward focus is that churches stop reaching non-churchgoers because they are less frequently meeting the needs of those outside of their fellowship.

Most non-churchgoers will avoid an ingrown church altogether because it does not appear to be sensitive to their needs. Even newly launched and emerging churches are not immune to becoming ingrown. The close fellowship created in new church plants, multiple-site churches, cell churches, art churches, café churches, and house churches often subtly redirect the leaders' attention inward and away from their mission fields.

Ask yourself, "How much of my volunteer time at church do I spend on meeting the needs of the congregation rather than meeting the needs of those who don't go to church?" If you do not see a balance, then the church you attend may be ingrown.

Good Churches Have This Problem Too

Ingrown churches actually arise for a good reason. A church's fellowship often is so attractive, compelling, and beneficial, that before long most of a congregation's attention becomes directed toward these benefits. Donald McGavran summed up these positive and negative attributes by saying a good church will create "redemption and lift."[2] By this he meant that once a person is redeemed (restored back to a relationship with God), the person's fellowship with other Christians will lift him or her away from previous friends who are non-churchgoers. The cure, according to McGavran, is to realize that this lift is good (it raises your life to a new level of loving Christ) but also bad (it separates you from non-churchgoers who need Christ's love too). McGavran argued that balance is needed in meeting the needs of those inside the church and those outside of it, and so does this chapter.

Good Reasons That Trap Churches into Ingrown Behavior

There are many reasons why churches gravitate toward an internal focus rather than an external one. In figure 1.1, let's look at four common church characteristics that, when left unattended, can unintentionally redirect a church into a closed, inward focus.

Figure 1.1: *Good Reasons That Trap Churches in Ingrown Behavior*	
(SELF-SCORING—Check all that apply)	
Does your church have a long history?	*The History Trap*
Does your church need to be better organized?	*The Organizational Trap*
Does your church have experienced volunteers?	*The Experience Trap*
Does your church have a sizable ministry to hurting people?	*The Infirmity Trap*

To understand figure 1.1, let's look at each trap more thoroughly.

The History Trap—*A Church with a Long History.* A church that is focused internally will eventually lose sight of its original mission and gravitate toward being an organization consumed with helping itself. Years and years of internal focus will result in a church that knows little else. Leaders raised in an internally focused church will think that the volunteer's role is to serve the existing congregation, perhaps to the point of burnout. Time erases the memory of the earliest days of a church conceived to meet the needs of non-churchgoers.

The Organizational Trap—*A Sizable Congregation That Must Be Managed.* Have you ever noticed that when new churches are started, they often have an outward focus? This may be because a newly planted church is often keenly aware that without reaching out to others, the new church will die. However, I have noticed that once a new church is about eighteen months old, it starts becoming so consumed with its organizational needs that it spends most of its time internally focused. Any church with a history over eighteen months long will usually be internally focused.

The Experience Trap—*A Church with a Talented and Long-Serving Team of Volunteers.*[3] When a church has a cadre of talented and gifted leaders, these volunteers are often asked to stay too long in their positions. They become regarded as experts by others and newcomers. The result is that leadership unintentionally becomes a closed clique, which newcomers with innovative ideas will often feel too intimidated to join.

The Infirmity Trap—*A Church with a Ministry to Hurting People.* Hurting people are often seeking to have their hurts healed by the soothing balm of Christian community. A church that is offering this is doing something good, because to help hurting people is what Christ calls his church to do (James 1:27). And a ministry to hurting people must be conducted with confidentiality and intimacy. An unintentional result of such confidentiality is that these churches can become closed communities too. Subsequently, churches often thwart their mission to reach out to the hurting and instead gravitate toward a closed fellowship where outsiders find it increasingly harder to get in and get the help they need.

SIGNS OF AN INGROWN CHURCH

Because positive church traits (such as closeness, long congregational histories, and talented volunteers) often inadvertently give rise to clan-like congregations, it is important to do a regular checkup to see if you have become ingrown in focus. Figure 1.2 lists several behaviors that researchers see as signs of an increasing internal focus. Ask yourself if some of these behaviors may be evident in your church.

Figure 1.2: *Signs of Ingrown Church Behavior*		
Behaviors of Ingrown Organizations[4]	*Signs*	*Behaviors of Ingrown Churches*
Leaders become the most valued asset in the organization, often unintentionally giving off a sense of elitism.	*Confidence* Organizational leadership is overly self-confident.	Leaders and church people subtly give off a sense that they have superior insight when compared to non-churchgoers.
Serving the organization is more important than serving the people within it.	*Importance* The organization has become more important than its people.	Volunteers are urged to ignore personal and family needs for the sake of serving the organization.[5]
Leaders try to control others because the mission and needs of the organization are so important.	*Power* People should be controlled for the sake of the organization mission and survival.	Church leaders persistently stress the importance of the organization's mission. This subtly insinuates the organization's needs should take precedence over family and personal needs.
Leaders change course often, casting aside volunteers in a desperate attempt to make the organization healthier.	*Planning* All planning centers around the needs of the organization. Experts control planning.	Churches experiment with many new ideas without assessing suitability or gaining feedback from volunteers, because the health of the organization is more critical than the health of the leaders.

So, how are you doing? You can assess your status with figure 1.3, because there is a difference between an internally focused church and one that is balanced with equal emphasis upon internal and external needs. Figure 1.3 gives examples of churches that are growing inward or outward. Check all that apply to your church. The column with the most checks may indicate whether your church is growing in, growing out, or is equally balanced (the goal of an uncommon church).

Figure 1.3: *How Many Ingrown Behaviors Does Our Church Exhibit?*	
(SELF-SCORING—Check all that apply)	
Growing In	*Growing Out*
☐ Our church sponsors events for the community but few community residents attend.	☐ Our paid staff spends over fifteen hours a week involved in non-church-related community work.
☐ My closest friends are also churchgoers.	☐ I regularly ask non-churchgoing people about what they are reading.
☐ Our church leaders spend most of their time focusing on church needs.	☐ When our church sponsors community events, about half the attendees are non-churchgoers.
☐ Our church has a daycare and/or preschool but few parents attend our church.	☐ I vacation with non-churchgoing friends.
☐ New people have moved into the neighborhood, and I invite them to church.	☐ New people have moved into the neighborhood, and I call them to ask how I can help.
☐ We have an outreach committee or person with the responsibility of reaching out to others.	☐ Our church has a job-training program for the under-employed.
☐ My recreational activities are usually with fellow Christians.	☐ Our church is known in the community for initiating many benevolence programs that have helped the needy.
☐ We do not have our own programs, but we support a lot of community-run benevolence programs.	☐ At our church, you will find volunteers who are not yet Christians, but who are attracted to the church because of our focus on meeting needs.
☐ Our church often argues about money, styles of music, or leadership decisions.	☐ When we have community events, we do not charge for food, etc.
☐ Our adult Sunday schools are usually comprised of those who have attended the church for many years.	☐ We have twelve-step groups that are attended by many regular church attendees.
Tally up the checks in this column. *TOTAL (growing IN):* _____	*Tally up the checks in this column.* *TOTAL (growing IN):* _____

EMBRACE THE CALL AND AVOID THE TRAPS

All of the traps that led to inward-focusing behaviors began with positive church traits. This means few churches today are immune from becoming inwardly focused. Therefore, a prescription for almost every church, even those that have recently grown or exhibited the above positive attributes, is to first embrace the call.

The call churches commonly follow leads to becoming an ingrown church. But isn't that growth OK? After all, it is growth in intimacy, closeness, and fellowship.

But Christ called his church to be something uncommonly more. Most notably, he called his church to assist him in reconnecting people to himself. Called the mission of God,[6] chapters 7 and 8 will help to discover how the uncommon church fosters this.

Jesus also emphasized that this call would include meeting the needs of those inside *and* outside his church. Jesus stressed this latter aspect of the call when he gave his disciples this guideline: "Here is a simple rule of thumb for behavior: Ask yourself what you want people to do for you; then grab the initiative and do it for them! If you only love the lovable, do you expect a pat on the back? Run-of-the-mill sinners do that. . . . I tell you, love your enemies. Help and give without expecting a return. You'll never—I promise—regret it" (Luke 6:31–33, 35 MSG).

James warned the early New Testament church that it was becoming ingrown and must immediately bring balance to their call with a renewed focus on the "homeless and loveless." James boldly cautioned: "Anyone who sets himself up as 'religious' by talking a good game is self-deceived. This kind of religion is hot air and only hot air. Real religion, the kind that passes muster before God the Father, is this: Reach out to the homeless and loveless in their plight, and guard against corruption from the godless world" (James 1:26–27 MSG).

THE CURE: HOW TO GROW O.U.T.

Chapter 2 will address the cure for this inward focus, beginning with a short story that illustrates how easy it is for a congregation to get trapped with an inward focus.[7] In this story, good intentions and even better fellowship lifted a church up to a new level of spiritual harmony, but it also lifted it away from those who needed help.

2 | HOW DOES A CHURCH GROW O.U.T.?

Since some readers will have jumped from the Quick-Start Guide directly to this chapter, here is brief summary of chapter 1 which describes the why for this chapter's how:

1. Today it is common for churches to be ingrown (focusing most of their ministry inward toward the needs of congregants).

2. Even good churches have this problem, because an advantage of Christian fellowship is the closeness it fosters. This closeness unintentionally draws focus from the needs of non-churchgoers.

3. God's call to his church is for her to meet the needs of non-churchgoers (Luke 6:31–35; James 1:26–27) by going out to them and reconnecting them to a loving heavenly Father. This is Christ's call (John 17:18).

4. The cure that will revitalize a common congregation and make it an uncommon one is a balance between inward ministry

(meeting the needs of churchgoers) and outward ministry (meeting the needs of non-churchgoers).

ST. GEORGE MEETS HIS MATCH AT ST. MARK'S

George was a likable man with high hopes for his pastorate at St. Mark's Church. The church had been founded some sixty years earlier to reach the sprawling new neighborhoods of the area. In the years after World War II, the church grew as young families with good jobs spread into the neat streets and shaded culs-de-sac.

Sometime after 1970, the church started to plateau in attendance. The neighborhood streets were now filled with nice and tidy homes, but even newer subdivisions began to sprout eight miles to the north. Because of its size of four hundred members, St. Mark's still enjoyed a favorable reputation in the denomination and few saw the plateau as troubling.

In the 1980s, a new emerging middle class of Korean-Americans began to move into the neighborhood. "I've got many neighbors who are Korean," stated one church board member. "They are good friends of mine. But, once they visit our church, they don't come back. I thought Pastor George would be the answer."

George was a Korean-American who had successfully grown a large church of the same denomination in Rosemead, California. The board of St. Mark's Church had felt that George would help them reach out to their neighbors. And try George did. George spent many hours walking the nearby streets and culs-de-sac asking residents about their needs: One pressing need was for after-school programs for children of families with both parents working. Another need was for Sunday school programs that would appeal to youth.

To meet this need, George tirelessly launched into a Wednesday after-school program and two new Sunday school classes. "I got the best workers and most experienced volunteers of the church to help me," recalled George. "But I never expected this." The church board had called the district superintendent and requested a different pastor. "We tried to reach the community," summarized George, "but it was just me who had the vision. The church's leaders had a burden in their minds, but not in their hearts. I guess they only heard about the neighborhood's needs secondhand, through me. I should have taken them with me to walk the neighborhood themselves."

It was this conversation with a wise pastor almost two decades ago that launched me on a quest to discover why the common church has trouble connecting with the communities around it. Over the years, I discovered that well-meaning pastors like George were insufficiently equipped to connect a church with the burgeoning needs of non-churchgoers. The task is too large for a staff to manage. Rather, for a church to be uncommon today, it will be necessary for all congregants to go out into their neighborhoods and connect with the needs of non-churchgoing people.

The story above still occurs. New churches are being planted that within a few years succumb to the same problems that St. Mark's Church experienced. They have different names, but they still fall prey to the same marginalizing commonness. Yet, as I counsel these congregations, I find that most churches genuinely want to reach out to those outside their fellowship. They intuitively (and biblically) know that Christ calls them to reach inward *and* outward. But they are at a loss to stem the tide. They are in need of a cure for the commonness of ingrown ministry.

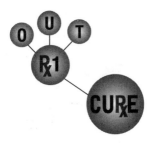

℞1 FOR THE COMMON CHURCH = GROW O.U.T.

The cure for the ingrown church is to keep the church focused both inwardly and outwardly. In fact, history indicates that churches that stay connected to outsiders often do a better job at inward ministry too. For example, an Anglican pastor named John Wesley was so ashamed and alarmed at the depravity of the people outside his church, that he took his sermons outside the church walls and began ministries to better serve their spiritual and physical needs.[1] Balancing this emphasis on people inside and outside the church required a rigorous structure his critics mockingly called "Wesley's Methods." Soon his followers were known as "Methodists," a term that endures today and should remind us that we need a clear method if we are going to avoid focusing only on people inside the church. I believe this method consists of three organic remedies. These cures, if taken together, can foster a healthy balance between inward and outward focus.

In this cure, and in all of the cures in this book, the remedies spell the name of the cure:

- **CURE O:** Observe whom you are equipped to reach.
- **CURE U:** Understand the needs of those you are equipped to reach.
- **CURE T:** Tackle needs by refocusing, creating, or ending ministry programs.

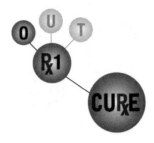

CU℞E O = OBSERVE WHOM YOU ARE EQUIPPED TO REACH

The main reason most churches become common is because they forget (or sometimes just don't know) to whom God has equipped them to reach out and minister.[2] They know they aren't supposed to be ingrown, but exactly who should they be growing out to serve? Usually, there are two options. The answer can be discovered by asking two questions:

1. Has God equipped your church to minister to people in a geographic community?

- If you answered yes, you might be a geographic church.
- *Geo-* means "of an area." This is a church whose ministry has been directed toward people in a geographic area (often those who live nearby).
- These churches meet the needs of people in one or more geographic communities.
- Examples might be a neighborhood church, a village church, a rural church, a church in a housing development, or a downtown church (see figure 2.1).

2. Has God equipped your church to minister to people like you?

- If you answered yes, you might be a demographic church.

- *Demo-* means "of a people." This is a church whose ministry has been directed toward a people group (those who share common characteristics).
- These churches meet the needs of one or more sections of the population that share common characteristics, such as age, ethnicity, and socioeconomics.[3]
- Examples might be generational churches, ethnic churches, aging traditional churches, blue-collar churches, middle-class churches, café churches, and college churches (see figure 2.2.)

Your road to becoming an uncommon church begins with understanding whether you are a church equipped to meet the needs of a specific geographic area, or you are more equipped to minister to one or more demographic sections of the population. Both geographic and demographic churches are legitimate and needed. The process begins by observing your surroundings, history, and how God has moved in your church's history.[4]

Are You a Geographic Church?

Some churches are primarily equipped by God to reach a geographic area such as a neighborhood, borough, small town, rural area, township, neighborhood, school district, suburb, or urban district. Geographic churches often have a long history of ministering in a specific area. And if the culture of the geographic area changes, because the geographic church is called to that locale, the geographic church will stay put and change with that culture.

Today, many churches are forced by their location or history to be geographic churches. Figure 2.1 lists some more common examples of geographic churches.

Figure 2.1: *Examples of Geographic Churches*	
Churches constrained[5] by *distance*	• Churches located in small towns and/or rural districts with very little outside traffic may have no other option than to become geographic churches meeting the needs of those people living nearby. • Churches that are elsewhere off the beaten path.
Churches constrained by *natural features*	• Churches located in wilderness, valleys, or other isolated areas with very little outside traffic. • Churches located in back-road areas. • Churches located on river deltas, islands, or peninsulas.
Churches constrained by *traffic patterns*	• Suburban churches may be geographic churches if they are in an area of a suburb not traveled by many people from outside of the area. • Churches can be geographic churches if their buildings are hidden in a housing development or subdivision.
Churches constrained by *owned assets*	• Churches that own their facilities (and market or geographic conditions make selling and moving impractical). • Churches that own significant or valuable acreage (and market or geographic conditions make selling and moving impractical).
Churches constrained by *image*	• Churches that are located in a neighborhood with its own identity (blue-collar, artist, urban, young professional, college student, or other). • An old, established downtown church that cannot move to the suburbs because there are other denominational churches already there. • A church residing in one of the inner city's labyrinth of neighborhoods may be limited by that neighborhood's identity.

Special Attributes of Geographic Churches

Geographic Churches Will Stay Put and Change as the Cultures around Them Change. If the cultural makeup of a community changes, a geographic church will change to reflect those changes. Rather than moving out of an area if the culture changes (like a demographic church might do), the geographic church is a chameleon, staying put and changing its appearances to reflect its changing environment.

Geographic Churches Can Reach Out to Several Cultures at the Same Time. A geographic church in an urban area might be comprised of a Mexican congregation, an Asian congregation, and a young professionals congregation.

There Is Power in Multicultural Geographic Churches. Because a geographic church wants to mirror the changing mosaic of its locale, geographic churches often seek to create a partnership of multiple sub-congregations, reflecting the proportions of these cultures in the community. These churches are discovering the power of partnership, for while some community residents may be leaving the area, geographic churches are reaching out to emerging groups that are moving into the area.

Geographic Churches May Be the Majority of Churches Today. From figure 2.1, we can see that most churches today may be geographically limited and thus are best able to reach out to their geographic communities.

Now let's look at another increasingly popular option, demographic churches.

Are You a Demographic Church?[6]

Today, people will drive a great distance to attend a church they like. As a result, more churches are drawing people from several sections of the population rather than just ministering to those in the geographic area nearby.

Demographic groups are sections of the population that talk alike, behave alike, and in which members can tell who is in their group and who is not.[7] Though the names and designations are always evolving, figure 2.2 highlights some examples of demographic churches.

Figure 2.2: *Examples of Demographic Churches*[8]	
Generational churches[9]	• Senior adult (b. 1945 and before) churches[10] also called "silent generation" or "builder generation" churches[11] • Boomer (b. 1946–1964) churches • Generation X (b. 1965–1983) churches • Generation Y (b. 1984–2002) churches
Socioeconomic churches[12]	• Churches in working-class neighborhoods • Urban churches among the working poor • Middle-class suburban churches
Ethnic churches[13]	• Latin-American churches • Hispanic-American churches • African-American churches • Asian-American churches • Native-American churches • Caucasian churches[14]
Affinity churches (focused around a common interest)	• Cowboy churches • NASCAR churches • Motorcycle churches • Emerging postmodern churches • Café churches • Art churches • College churches[15]

Special Attributes of Demographic Churches

Demographic Churches Can Reach Out to Several Cultures at the Same Time. Like geographic churches, a demographic church could be comprised of a Latino/Latina congregation, an Asian congregation, an aging retiree congregation, and an emerging postmodern congregation.

There Is Power in Multicultural Geographic Churches. When a demographic church sees a people group on the wane (senior adults, for example), it often intentionally reaches out to an emerging demographic such as young professionals or young postmodern adults. Unlike the geographic church, whose decision on who to reach is guided by who is coming into the area, the demographic church focuses on an advantageous demographic.

Demographic Churches Will Change Locations, Following a People Group as it Moves to New Locales. If the demographic group it is reaching moves out of the area, a demographic church moves along with the culture. For example, a Boomer church may move from an urban area to the suburbs as its congregants move to those suburbs. And an Asian church I know moved to a nearby town when most of its Asian members moved to that town.

Can Churches Be Geographic and Demographic?

Yes! Many churches are reaching nearby geographic areas, as well as several far-flung demographics. In fact, this may be one of the healthiest ways for a church to grow, because the church maintains a strong local ministry while reaching out to more distant people groups. Such congregations create a wonderful region-wide ministry coupled with a strong local foundation.

St. Thomas' Church in Sheffield, England, is a good example of a demographic church that has a robust ministry to its local geographic area. England's largest Anglican church (where most churchgoers are under the age of thirty-five) calls itself "a church of churches," with worship services at different locations around town for varying people groups (for example, a young professionals church, a student church, a church for internationals, and different churches in different neighborhoods). It also has a robust local ministry in the geographic area of its first church, called the Mother Church. This Mother Church was the original Anglican congregation that gave rise to "a church of [six] churches" around town.[16]

For many small churches, being both geographic and demographic may not be an option. Because the average church in North America is only seventy-five attendees,[17] most of these churches do not have the numbers to be both geographic and demographic. Thus, the common church in North America must first determine if it is called to stay put and reach out to its geographic area, or if it is called to move and follow a people group it has been reaching. Figure 2.3 will be the key to determining this.

Which Church Are You?

Use figure 2.3 to investigate what type of church God has equipped you to be. Neither the geographic approach nor the demographic approach is better than the other. They are simply two ways that God equips his church to reach out. Each approach has pros and cons (see figure 2.4).

The starting place is to look at your history, situation, and under what circumstances God moves in your midst. To begin this process, check the boxes in the columns of figure 2.3 that most represent your church and its vision.

Figure 2.3: *Are You a Geographic or Demographic Church?*		
	You might be a Geographic Church if . . .	*You might be a Demographic Church[18] if . . .*
Focus	☐ You have a burden to reach a geographic area for Christ. ☐ Needs in a geographic area or neighborhood dictate your ministry.	☐ You have a burden to reach one or more people groups for Christ. ☐ The needs of certain people groups (which may be spread across a region) dictate your ministry.
Pastor	☐ Your pastor feels called to your geographic community. ☐ Your pastor has stayed (or is planning to stay) for a long time in the church's geographical area.	☐ Your pastor feels called to a certain people (ethnic, generational, etc., see figure 2.2). ☐ Your pastor is open to moving out of the area if most of the church's attendees live or are moving out of the area.
Staff	☐ Most of the church staff live in the church's geographical area. ☐ Most of the staff have long histories in the church's geographical area.	☐ Most of the church staff does not live in the church's geographical area. ☐ Most of the church staff does not have a long history in the church's geographical area.
Facilities	☐ Your church owns permanent facilities in the area. ☐ In the past five years you have built new facilities in the area. ☐ In the past five years you have renovated or updated facilities.	☐ You change facilities as need arises, leasing or renting church facilities rather than owning them. ☐ You have multiple auditoriums or venues to accommodate different worship styles.

continued

Figure 2.3: *Are You a Geographic or Demographic Church?* continued		
	You might be a Geographic Church if . . .	You might be a Demographic Church if . . .
Limiting Factors	☐ Your location is hemmed in by geographic features that sometimes thwart visitors from finding you, such as: • A valley, hill, or river; • A small town surrounded by farmland; • A neighborhood with its own identity.	☐ Your churchgoers are aging. ☐ Your churchgoers are moving away from the area to an area where there are churches similar to yours that they may attend.
Characteristics	☐ Your church is in a small town. ☐ Your church is in a neighborhood that has a specific identity. ☐ Your church is in an urban area of a city.	☐ Your church is in a middle-class suburban neighborhood. ☐ Your church is a church with attendees primarily under the age of thirty-five. ☐ Your church is known for blending several people groups together.[19]
Names	☐ Your church name reflects the geographic area you are called to reach, such as • Smithville Church • Pine Lake Church • First (i.e., downtown) Church • Harris Avenue Church, etc. ☐ Your church name has not been changed in a long time.	☐ Your church name reflects the language of a people group, such as: • Overcomers' Church • Family Worship Center • Community Church[20] • A Greek or Latin name (e.g., The Crux; Latin for *cross*; or *Missio Dei*). ☐ Your church name has been changed in the last decade.
Growth	☐ Your church experienced a period of growth between 1950 and 1970.	☐ Your church experienced a period of growth since 1970.
Results	Total: _____	Total: _____
	(If you have equal checks in both columns you may be geographic and demographic church)[21]	

When you tally the columns in figure 2.3, you will begin to see a congregational trajectory. But remember, there are strengths and weaknesses to each approach. In figure 2.4, write down which demographic or geographic area you are called to reach.

Figure 2.4: *Whose Needs Are You Called to Meet?* *(Circle one)*	
A geographic area (describe it here)	Demographic groups (describe it/them here)
Remember these pros and cons:	
Pros of geographic church: • Builds a strong connection with an area. • Can more readily bring about racial and cultural reconciliation within a changing area.[22] • Does not need to move facilities as often. • Can invest in local facilities enjoying ownership privileges. *Cons of geographic church:* • Encounters change more often because geographic areas regularly experience cultural transitions. • Staff and leaders usually do not stay for a long time, rather transitioning in and out as the culture changes.	*Pros of demographic church:* • Builds a strong communication connection with sections of the population that share common characteristics. • Provides relevant ministry. • Can move with a people group, leasing or renting facilities in lieu of purchasing or building them. • Encounters change less often. • Staff can remain a long time. *Cons of demographic church:* • Can become culturally prejudiced. • Can become separatist (i.e., siloed) unless it grows into a church where different people groups partner in the same church.[23]

For More Information Read:
• Appendix 2.A: "Examples of Churches Called to a Community or Called to a Demographic"
• Appendix 2.B: "John Perkins' 3 Rs: How Mono-Demographic Churches Can Help Urban Congregations"

Figure 2.4 should give you a general indication of the direction of your church's recent ministry.[24] Before you move ahead to the next remedy, it is important to reflect back on what kind of church God has equipped you to be.

CU℞ U = UNDERSTAND THE NEEDS OF THOSE YOU ARE EQUIPPED TO REACH

Many churches simply stop after determining who they are equipped to reach. But the cure for the common church is not complete until you finish the entire regimen. And, **CU℞ U** is the most important aspect of this prescription, for here you will discover the needs of non-churchgoing people (of the geographic community or demographic you are equipped to reach).

The best way to do this is simply to ask. But, as we saw earlier, the road to health requires a method, and **CU℞ U** includes:

- Selecting a suitable question to ask in order to ascertain needs.
- Selecting a suitable time and place to ask this question.
- Mapping out a master list of needs.

Selecting a Suitable Question to Ask

Canvassing an area or a demographic about its needs must be done with respect, discretion, and confidentiality. Below are principles that will guide you.

Ask a Nonintrusive Question. Some readers may wonder, "Can't we just come out point-blank and ask them about their needs?" This is often too invasive. Discretion is needed since people often consider spiritual matters when they are experiencing a crisis in life.[25] They sense that a Christian community can provide the solace, comfort, and help they seek. They also do not want that assistance to come from a stranger but from a friend. Therefore, though they are interested in spiritual matters, they will usually not yet be ready to talk about that predicament openly.

Herein lies the dilemma. People want to open up and share with you about their needs, but they are not ready to do so until they have a relationship with you and can trust you.

The key to building a relationship while not being too invasive is to *not* ask about their needs (this will often be too personal at first). Rather, ask about what they see as needs in their community or demographic. When asked this way, they will usually tell you about their needs. For example, one young lady shared with a canvasser, "Our community needs after-school programs to keep children from getting in trouble." Later the congregant discovered that this lady was struggling with her own children and the trouble they caused between the time they got home and when she returned home after work. A young couple told another client, "People need better jobs around here so they don't have to work two jobs just to make ends meet." The church discovered many of the young people in the neighborhood had been laid off from a nearby factory so it began a career counseling ministry.

Figure 2.5 is a sample question you can modify as needed to ask about the needs of others.

Figure 2.5: *Canvass Question*

Sample

> "Hello. My name is _____ (name) and I am from _____ (name of church). I am asking people to help us understand what are the greatest needs of this community that a church like ours could address.

Now, rewrite the survey question of figure 2.5, being sensitive to your local geographic or demographic context. Put your modified survey question in the appropriate box of figure 2.6.

Selecting a Suitable Time and Place to Ask

Because this asking must also be done at a nonintrusive time and place, you must meet two criteria.

Ask at a Convenient Time. Sunday morning between ten and noon continues to be a time when most non-churchgoing people have free time in their schedule. Therefore, you may need to allow your canvassers to skip the morning service or Sunday school hour to undertake a canvass at this time. The second least chaotic time during the week is Saturday morning from ten to noon. This can be a good second choice.

Ask at a Convenient Place. Are you called to reach a geographic area? Then the answer is simple: Determine the geographic area and ask around the area. Are you called to reach a demographic? Here the question is more complex. Meet with the canvassers in advance and ask, "Where can we connect with people of our demographic?"

Add to figure 2.6 the time and place where you will conduct your canvass.

Figure 2.6: *Canvass Question, Time, and Place*	
Our Canvass Question	
(fill in your survey question here)	
"Hello . . .	
Time for Canvassing of Needs	Place for Canvassing of Needs
First choice:	First choice:
Second choice:	Second choice:

Mapping Out a Master List of Needs

While canvassers are talking to individuals, they should ask permission to jot down notes. Let them know this is because you value their input. However, do not write down their names or ask if they want to be contacted regarding ministries launched to meet these needs. If you launch a ministry that meets their needs, they will hear about it. Figure 2.7 shows how mapping out of needs can be conducted.

Now that you have mapped out needs, it is important to sort out these needs into recurring categories. This will be done under **CU$_X$RE T**.

Figure 2.7: *Mapping Out Needs (a sample)*[26]
Column 1 (used again in figure 2.8)
A list of needs jotted down while listening to the interviewee.
Person 1 (sample) • Job training program because many are under-employed. • A class offering English as a second language. • A coat exchange to provide winter clothing.
Person 2 (sample) • Financial budgeting seminars. • After-school program for kids. • School supplies and backpacks.
Person 3 (sample) • Help with parenting strong-willed teens. • Place where youth could come on the weekend to stay out of trouble.
Person 4 (sample) • Transportation to the doctor. • Health advice and advocacy.

CU$_X$RE T = TACKLE NEEDS BY REFOCUSING, CREATING, OR ENDING MINISTRY PROGRAMS

The term *tackle* is fitting, because this may require the most energy of the three cures in this chapter. As we saw earlier, long histories and good fellowship often cause a church to focus on congregational needs in lieu of non-churchgoer needs. Thus, churchgoers often focus on ministries they enjoy doing even when these programs are no longer meeting the needs of non-churchgoers. As a result, CU**R**E T is absolutely critical for church health. Three tactics will be needed:

- Refocusing: Some of a church's programs will need to be refocused to better meet the needs of non-churchgoers.
- Creating: Some programs will need to be created to meet the needs of non-churchgoers.
- Ending: Some programs will need to end so that volunteers and assets can be redeployed into programs that better serve the needs of non-churchgoers.

Refocusing and Creating Ministries: The A-B-C-D Approach

The key to refocusing or creating ministry is to:

A. Assemble both canvassers and ministry leaders.

- The goal is to compile a master list of needs and draw connections to existing ministries or create new ministries that will meet those needs.
- A convener (chairperson) should be selected. This will usually be a staff person or the leader of the canvassers. He or she will oversee the A-B-C-D steps.
- Convene both canvassers and church ministry leaders as soon as possible after the canvassing. Some churches will conduct their canvass on Sunday or Saturday morning and then meet that afternoon. This can allow leaders to consider the results while the conversations are fresh in their minds.

B. Brainstorm a master list of needs.

- When the canvassers convene after their canvass, everyone shares the needs.

- From these lists, create a master list of needs (of those that reoccur with the most frequency on the canvassers' lists).
- Combine similar needs into categories.
- Column 2 of figure 2.8 illustrates how a master list of needs might be categorized from the sample in figure 2.7.

C. Correlate needs to ministries the church offers or can start.

- Just as you brainstormed a master list of categories, now it is time to brainstorm a list of ministries you can refocus or launch to meet needs in each category.
- Put these ministry ideas in column 3 of figure 2.8.

Figure 2.8: Correlate Needs with Ministry Ideas		
Column 1	Column 2	Column 3
A list of needs jotted down while listening to the interviewee *(from figure 2.7)*	Master list of needs and brainstormed solutions	Refocused or created ministry ideas to meet these needs
Person 1 (sample) • Job training program because many are under-employed. • A class offering English as a second language. • A coat exchange to provide winter clothing.	**Need A: Better jobs** *Solutions:* • Job training program. • A class offering English as a second language. • Financial budgeting seminars.	*(list ministries that could be refocused/created here)* A. B. C.
Person 2 (sample) • Financial budgeting seminars. • After-school program for kids. • School supplies and backpacks. Person 3 (sample) • Help with parenting strong-willed teens. • Place where youth could come on the weekend to stay out of trouble.	**Need B: Help with youth and children** *Solutions:* • A coat exchange to provide winter clothing. • Afterschool program for children. • Help with parenting strong-willed teens. • School supplies and backpacks. • Place where youth could come on the weekend to stay out of trouble	D. E. F. G. *continued*

Figure 2.8: *Correlate Needs with Ministry Ideas continued*

Column 1	Column 2	Column 3
Person 4 (sample) • Transportation to the doctor. • Health advice and advocacy.	**Need C: Assistance with health problems** *Solutions:* • Recovery/support groups for addiction or damaging behavior. • Parish nurse program. • Hygiene and/or dietary counseling.	H. I. J.

D. **D**istribute your list of refocused or created ministries (figure 2.8) to church leaders.

- Send this list to all department heads and ministry leaders.
- Ask them to look over your suggestions in column 3 of figure 2.8 and add their own suggestions.
- Ask them to report back in thirty days with their responses of how their ministry can be refocused to better meet community needs.
- The report will be received by the staff person or convener who oversees the canvass.

Ending Ministry: Three Guidelines

As noted, some ministries may need to end. This is especially important when volunteers need to be redeployed into ministries that better meet the needs of non-churchgoers.

One example comes from a client church. This church had a group of ladies that met Wednesday afternoons to knit blankets, which they sold to raise funds for missionaries. The missionaries were appreciative, but the efforts raised little funds. The ladies mostly enjoyed the fellowship and felt they were supporting outreach. A canvass of the community found that many of the families with two wage earners needed after-school child care. Armed with this information, the leader of the canvass asked the Wednesday knitting group to consider hosting a tutor and play time from 3 to 5:30 once a month (the time during which they typically knitted). Community residents and children so enjoyed these afternoons with their newly adopted "grandmas" (and the senior ladies enjoyed it, too) that this ministry soon replaced the weekly knitting circle.

Still, there are three guidelines that must be adhered to when ending a ministry and redeploying volunteer skills.

Guideline 1: Redeploy People. Volunteers involved in a ministry that is ending must clearly see a redeployment for their skills and fellowship. The knitting circle became an afterschool team of surrogate grandmas. At first the knitting circle was hesitant, but once the members saw that their skills and fellowship would be preserved, they relinquished one ministry to launch another.

Guideline 2: Move Slowly. Most people will need time to process the end of their ministries as well as the value of diverting their skills. One of the key lessons of research into church change is that leaders often doom the change process by proceeding too quickly (by not giving congregants enough time to grapple with the change).[27]

Guideline 3: Add if You Can't Subtract. If you can't end it, leave it, and add something else. Some people are so wrapped up in their ministries that they cannot envision ever doing anything else. While it might not be the most desirable tactic, if ending a ministry is causing too much division or grief, it is best to leave the ministry alone and launch something new. Many church leaders have become bogged down trying to end something when that energy might have been better spent launching something new.

Fill in figure 2.9 to ensure you meet all three guidelines when ending a ministry.

Figure 2.9: *Guidelines for Ending a Ministry*

Describe the ministry that may need to be ended:

List leaders and volunteers involved:

	Guideline 1: Redeploy people
How will volunteers see a redeployment for their skills and fellowship?	
	Guideline 2: Move slowly
How will we move slowly?	
	Guideline 3: Add if you can't subtract
If we can't end it, at what point will we leave it and add something else?	

Ending a ministry may be the most difficult and thorny task you undertake in growing a church O.U.T. So remember, if ending a ministry becomes too problematic, it is best to let it begin something new.

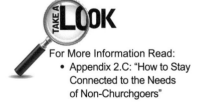

For More Information Read:
- Appendix 2.C: "How to Stay Connected to the Needs of Non-Churchgoers"

CONCLUSION

That's it! ℞1 for the common church is to grow O.U.T. with the following structure:

- **CURE O:** Observe whom you are equipped to reach.
- **CURE U:** Understand the needs of those you are equipped to reach.
- **CURE T:** Tackle needs by refocusing, creating, or ending ministry programs.

Follow the above remedies and you will be on your way to getting out of an ingrown rut and back to meeting the needs of those who do not yet have a relationship with Jesus Christ.

QUESTIONS FOR GROUP AND PERSONAL REFLECTION

CURE O = OBSERVE WHOM ARE YOU EQUIPPED TO REACH

Question 1: Who Are You Equipped to Reach—Christians, Certain Geographic Areas, or Specific Demographics?

Begin this process by revising your results to the following figures. If you are doing this as a group, compare your answers in figures 2.3 and 2.4 with the answers of your group. Draft an initial compromise statement in figures 2.10 and 2.11.

Figure 2.10: *Is Your Church a Geographical or a Demographic Church?*	
My personal answers:	
You might be a Geographic Church if . . .	You might be a Demographic Church if . . .
(total checked in this column)	(total checked in this column)
	continued

Figure 2.10: *Is Your Church a Geographical or a Demographic Church?* continued

Group composite answers:	
You might be a Geographic Church if . . .	You might be a Demographic Church if . . .
(total checked in this column)	(total checked in this column)

Figure 2.11: *Whose Needs Are You Called to Meet?* (Circle one)

Personal answers or group composite answers:	
a geographic community (describe it here)	a demographic (describe it here)

CURE U = UNDERSTAND THE NEEDS OF THOSE YOU ARE EQUIPPED TO REACH

Question 2: What Are the Needs of Those You Are Equipped to Reach?

If you are doing this as a group, compare your personal answers in figure 2.6 with the answers from the group. Are there differences?

Compile your answers and put them in figure 2.12.

Select a canvassing group from among your study group, fellow churchgoers, and church volunteers. It is best to not use paid staff among the canvassers, but to let laypeople do the canvassing.[28] Utilizing laity can overcome a perception that only the staff, and not the greater part of the congregation, is interested in knowing non-churchgoer needs.

Agree to canvass the geographic area or demographic you are equipped to reach in the next thirty days. List in figure 2.12 the time, places, question, and participants.

Select a convener and a secretary for this canvassing (job descriptions follow figure 2.12).

Figure 2.12: *Canvass Question, Time, and Place with Participant List*

Convener:	Secretary:

Time of Canvassing of Needs . . .	*Place of Canvassing of Needs . . .*
First choice:	First choice:
Second choice:	Second choice:

Our canvass question . . .

"Hello . . .

(fill in your survey question here)

Canvass Participants*:*   (Circle the chairperson and secretary)

1. _____ *(name)*
   _____ *(e-mail)*
   _____ *(church involvement)*
   _____ *(phone)*

2. _____ *(name)*
   _____ *(e-mail)*
   _____ *(church involvement)*
   _____ *(phone)*

3. _____ *(name)*
   _____ *(e-mail)*
   _____ *(church involvement)*
   _____ *(phone)*

4. _____ *(name)*
   _____ *(e-mail)*
   _____ *(church involvement)*
   _____ *(phone)*

5. _____ *(name)*
   _____ *(e-mail)*
   _____ *(church involvement)*
   _____ *(phone)*

6. _____ *(name)*
   _____ *(e-mail)*
   _____ *(church involvement)*
   _____ *(phone)*

7. _____ *(name)*
   _____ *(e-mail)*
   _____ *(church involvement)*
   _____ *(phone)*

continued

Figure 2.12: *Canvass Question, Time, and Place with Participant List* continued

Canvass Participants: (Circle the chairperson and secretary)

8. _____ *(name)*
_____ *(e-mail)*
_____ *(church involvement)*
_____ *(phone)*

9. _____ *(name)*
_____ *(e-mail)*
_____ *(church involvement)*
_____ *(phone)*

10. _____ *(name)*
_____ *(e-mail)*
_____ *(church involvement)*
_____ *(phone)*

11. _____ *(name)*
_____ *(e-mail)*
_____ *(church involvement)*
_____ *(phone)*

12. _____ *(name)*
_____ *(e-mail)*
_____ *(church involvement)*
_____ *(phone)*

Job Descriptions
The Convener Will

- Schedule, organize, and chair the canvass itself and follow-up meetings to discuss results.
- Follow up with ministry heads and department leaders to ensure that recommendations from the canvassing group for refocusing, creating, or ending ministry programs are considered.

The Secretary Will

- Notify participants of all meetings.
- Assist the convener in scheduling and organizing the canvass along with subsequent meetings.
- Write down the results of the canvass and meetings, distributing them to appropriate church departments.

The Canvass Participants Will

- Canvass the community.
- Assemble a master list of needs.
- Each year, meet monthly (over one quarter immediately before the "annual checkup" described on pp. 160–167) to review reports from church departments regarding what they are doing to address the needs that canvassers identified.

CURE T = TACKLE NEEDS BY REFOCUSING, CREATING, OR ENDING MINISTRY PROGRAMS

Question 3: What Ministry(ies) Should We Refocus, Create, or End to Better Meet Needs?

The key to refocusing, creating, or ending ministry is the A-B-C-D approach.

Assemble Both Canvassers and Ministry Leaders.

- Who will do this? _____
  (Write the name of the convener you selected here.)
- When will this meeting take place? _____
  (Write the date and time you selected.)

Brainstorm a Master List of Needs.

- At this meeting ask everyone to share the needs they discovered.
- Create a master list of needs that reoccur most often on the canvassers' lists (figure 2.13 below).
- Combine similar needs into categories.

Correlate Needs to Ministries the Church Offers or Can Start.

- Just as you brainstormed a master list of needs and categories, brainstorm a list of ministries you can refocus or launch to meet needs in each category.
- Put these ministry ideas in the correct column of figure 2.13.

Distribute Your List of Refocused or Created Ministries to Church Leaders.

- Send figure 2.13 to all department heads and ministry leaders.
- Ask them to look over your suggestions and add their own.
- Ask them to report back in thirty days with their responses of how ministry under their auspices can be refocused to better meet community needs.

Figure 2.13: Correlating Needs with Ministry Options		
Column 1	Column 2	Column 3
A list of needs jotted down while listening to the interviewee (from figure 2.7)	Master list of needs and brainstormed solutions	Refocused or created ministry ideas to meet these needs
Person 1	**Need A:** Solutions: • • •	(list ministries that could be refocused/created here) A. B. C.
Person 2	**Need B:** Solutions: • •	 D. E.
		continued

Figure 2.13: *Correlating Needs with Ministry Options* *continued*

Column 1	Column 2	Column 3
Person 3	• •	F. G.
Person 4	**Need C:** ———————— *Solutions:* • • •	H. I. J.

Question 4: What Ministries Might Need to End to Better Redeploy Volunteers?

Discuss frankly but with sensitivity which ministries may need to end. Use figure 2.14 to begin the discussion of ending ministries and to follow the three guidelines. Copy this figure and fill in the correct space for each ministry under consideration for closure.

Figure 2.14: *Three Guidelines for Ending Ministry*

Describe the ministry that may need to be ended:

List leaders and recipients:

Guideline 1: Redeploy people

How will volunteers see a redeployment for their skills and fellowship?

continued

Figure 2.14: *Three Guidelines for Ending Ministry* continued

	Guideline 2: Move slowly
How will we move slowly?	

	Guideline 3: Add if you can't subtract
If we can't end it, at what point will we leave it and add something else?	

Question 5 (optional): How Are You Staying Connected to the Needs of Non-Churchgoers?

What are you learning about the things non-churchgoers enjoy?

- What books are they reading and what is the message in those books?
- What TV shows and movies do they watch and why?
- What do they do on Sunday mornings when you are at church?
- What do they do for recreation?
- Where do they go on their vacations?

What are you learning about their daily lives?

- Where do they eat?
- Where do they buy their food?
- Where do they get their hair cut?
- Where do they buy their clothes?
- How do they get to work?

- Where is that "third place"[29] where they like to hang out that is neither work nor home?

What are you learning about their opinions on religion and God?

- Who do they perceive God to be?
- What kind of personality do they think God has?
- What kind of relationships do they wish they had with God?
- What are their philosophies of life?
- If they were leaning toward any one religion today, what would it be and why?

GROW S.M.A.L.L.

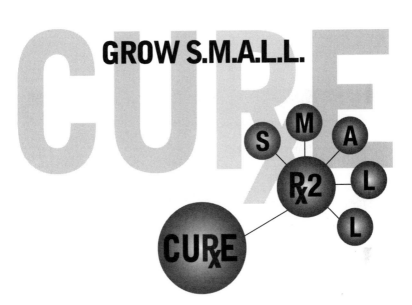

3 | WHY GROW S.M.A.L.L.?

"Yours may be a COMMON CHURCH if . . ."
(SELF-SCORING—Check all that apply)

☐ Your church is well-known for its weekend worship services.

☐ Your church is not meeting its budget.

☐ Your nominating committee has exhausted its circle of friends.

☐ You convinced your aunt to volunteer for the church council because she is the only person you know who hasn't been on it yet.

☐ Your church is known for engaging preaching.

☐ Your church musicians are more highly regarded than your Sunday school teachers.

☐ If you had a dire need, you would probably call the pastor first.

☐ Your pastor starts looking up Old Testament Scriptures when someone says, "I've got a new idea!"

☐ Your church is known for its attractive building and/or children's programs.

☐ Twenty percent of your attendees seem to be doing 80 percent of the work.

☐ Some of the people you know best at church are those who sit near you.

☐ Planning for weekend services takes 20 percent or more of your church staff's weekly time.

☐ You attend church but don't know many people well.

☐ Your closest friends attend another church.

THE COMMON CHURCH IS TOO BIG

Immediately when I make a statement like "The common church is too big," many readers will exclaim, "That cannot be true! A bigger church is more likely to survive in today's economic climate. And, a bigger church can have more resources, time, and talent to make a bigger impact."

Those protestations are right. In my own consulting work, I have estimated that a church today needs to average about 175 adult attendees in weekend worship for it to have the resources to offer the level of ministry that people expect today. Yet, many churches today are smaller than this. Some estimates are that the average church in North America has only around seventy-five adult attendees each weekend.[1]

And so, if the common church in America is less than half the size needed for sustainability, why would I recommend that churches get smaller? The key is focus. Where are today's churches focused? Are they focused on distinction and bigness? Or are they focused on intimacy and personal closeness? And are both foci possible? We will see shortly that both foci are possible, but first let's look at the attraction of bigness.

THE LURE OF BIG

Churches today are often focused on growing big. Some wonder if this occurred because the church growth movement seemed to emphasize bigness. Yet, if you look at the principles of church growth you will not find the culprit there, for the movement's founder emphasized it is not about big, but it's about effectiveness in making disciples.[2] Still, regardless of the reasons, the influence of large megachurches has resulted in many smaller congregations trying to copy the megachurch's attractive worship, programs, and facilities.

The problem is that most churches cannot (and should not) try to copy the attractive model of large mega-congregations.[3] If the American Religious Identification Survey is right and the median size for a church is seventy-five attendees,[4] then most churches are too small to muster the level of quality and service needed to grow with an "attractiveness" strategy. Many pastors, with dreams of mega impact, push their small congregations too hard toward attractive tactics when their church is really just too small to have the resources to compete.

Granted, some small churches can succeed with an attractiveness strategy, but most will not. An attractiveness strategy is not rooted in Jesus' example,[5] nor in case study research.[6] And researchers have found that an attractiveness strategy tends to create consumers, audiences, and church shoppers.[7]

THE CURE OF SMALL

We will see shortly that the cure for the common church, regardless of the church's size, is not an attraction strategy, but to become smaller. To become smaller means that a church increasingly focuses on the health of its small, intimate fellowship structures. And it begins by a church becoming small in its focus, structure, leaders, and emphasis.

But does an emphasis upon getting smaller make a church more healthy? I believe it does, for it is in small, intimate gatherings where most growth in Christian faith and maturity can take place. Let me explain.

Most people understand that according to Jesus' Great Commission (Matt. 28:19), a church's focus should be about spiritual growth and maturity, not about size, prestige, or status (more on this in the next chapter). And if growth in spiritual maturity is our goal, where is the best venue for that spiritual growth to be nurtured? Does spiritual maturity naturally flow out of the anonymity and detachment created in a large church event?[8] I have observed that it is difficult for spiritual growth to take place in large gatherings because questions are uncommon if not impractical, and personal dialogue about spiritual struggles is out of place.

Or perhaps it is in intimate, personal relationships that discipleship occurs. Leroy Eims in *The Lost Art of Disciplemaking* stated it well:

The ministry is to be carried on by people, not programs. It is to be carried out by *someone* and not by *some thing*. Disciples cannot be mass produced. We cannot drop people into a "program" and see disciples emerge at the end of a production line. It takes time to make disciples. It takes individual, personal attention. It takes hours of prayer for them. It takes patience and understanding to teach them how to get into the Word of God for themselves, how to feed and nourish their souls, and by the power of the Holy Spirit how to apply the Word to their lives. And it takes being an example to them of all of the above.[9]

Thus the best locale may be a small group of Christians helping one another deal with the struggles of their faith. Small fellowship groups have historically been the intimate environments where people can share their spiritual questions, religious doubts, pains, and aspirations. These compassionate environments allow people with problems to be more forthcoming and candid. To better understand the power of small to foster disciple-making, let's look at a few biblical and historical examples.

THE BIBLE AND SMALL FELLOWSHIP GROUPS

The most familiar small group in the Bible is Jesus' twelve disciples.[10] Jesus drew twelve followers closely to himself, training them for a mission that would one day surge across the Roman Empire and beyond (Matt. 4:18–22; Mark 3:13–19; Luke 6:13). In fact, in Jesus' time, synagogues were often small, and it was permissible to launch them with as few as ten men.[11] Jesus also utilized groups of seventy-two (Luke 10:1), but it was in his ongoing small fellowship of twelve disciples where Jesus addressed their most intimate and personal questions, problems, and needs. In this small group setting Jesus:

- Answered their questions about theology, history, and the future (Matt. 24:1–3);
- Modeled for his disciples healing and prayer; then gave them the power to go out and do likewise (Matt. 10:5–10); and
- Rebuked his disciples' wayward attitudes and ideas (Luke 16:13).

Finally, Hebrews 10:24–25 reminds us to "consider how we may spur one another on toward love and good deeds. Let us not give up meeting together, as some are in the habit of doing, but let us encourage one another—and all the more as you see the Day approaching." Many people use these verses to urge attendance at weekend church services, and this could certainly be one application. But the admonition here is to "spur one another on toward love and good deeds . . . encourage one another," which *can* happen at weekend church services, but in my observations is not likely. These verses apply even better to small group settings where spurring "one another on toward love and good deeds" and encouraging one another can more readily be accomplished.

JOHN WESLEY'S USE OF SMALL GROUPS[12]

One of history's most remarkable spiritual renewals took place when an unassuming Anglican pastor named John Wesley took his message outside the stately confines of English churches and into the streets. The message was so widely received that the teeming throngs of new converts began to overload the system.

In response, Wesley designed a system of small groups he called "class meetings" to help new converts begin the discipleship process. Not only did he require attendance in these small groups, but he also did not allow followers to attend the larger "society meetings" (similar to our weekend worship services) if they had not already attended their weekly small group. This would be akin to requiring congregants today to attend a small group during the week or they would not be allowed to attend weekend worship service. Think of how that might drive up small group attendance! One Cambridge University researcher declared, "The secret of the Methodist movement was its small groups."[13]

TODAY'S SMALL GROUP RENAISSANCE

Beginning in the early 1970s, the discipleship power of small groups led some Christians to make small groups their rallying cry. America started to notice the impact of small groups when the largest church in the world, a congregation in Seoul, South Korea, credited its phenomenal growth to its emphasis upon small groups.[14]

In North America, one of the first books to describe the power of small groups in a mainline church was by Presbyterian pastor Ray Stedman, who emphasized small groups as the discipleship hub of a "body life" church.[16] Many mainline churches were highly

> In his book *Surprising Insights from the Unchurched,* Thom Rainer declared, "New Christians who immediately became active in a small group are five times more likely to remain in the church five years later than those who were active in worship services alone."[15]

influenced by Stedman's approach, and small groups became a fashionable program within mainline congregations. Soon afterward the Vineyard churches, which combined an emphasis on small groups with charismatic expressions, ushering many Pentecostal and charismatic congregations into the small group movement.[17] Some churches called this small group emphasis "cell churches" because small groups should grow and divide like the human cell.[18] Other churches have used varied names for these small groups, including:

- Face-to-Face Groups (Lyle Schaller[19])
- Heart-to-Heart Groups (Kent Hunter[20])
- Kinship Circles (C. Peter Wagner[21])

- Life Cells (Eddie Gibbs[22])
- Growth Groups (Larry Osborne[23], Nelson Searcy, and Kerrick Thomas[24])
- Community Groups (Andy Stanley and Bill Willits[25])

Such small groups have been shown to be the glue that helps people stick with a Christian community. In his book *Surprising Insights from the Unchurched*, Thom Rainer declared, "New Christians who immediately became active [in a small group] were five times more likely to remain in the church five years later than those who were active in worship services alone."[26] And writer and pastor Larry Osborne calls a church with a healthy small group network a "sticky church," because congregants stick together and to the congregation.[27]

SMALL GROUP BACKLASH: "I'M NOT GETTING SMALLER; I'M BACKING AWAY FROM YOU"

When any new church strategy comes along, there are always those proponents who push too forcefully with a result that many become alienated to the new idea. In fact, researchers have discovered that pushing too strongly without building consensus usually dooms church change.[28] The small group emphasis is no exception. Because new ideas are often helpful, desperate church leaders grasping at anything to save a dying church will often move too quickly toward adapting a small group structure without first building consensus.

Other tactics that create backlash to small groups include past experiences with divisiveness of small groups and not recognizing that many congregants already attend some sort of small group, which means they don't have time for another one.

Appendix 3.A describes typical small group errors and how to overcome them. If you have experienced disunity, inward focus, not enough good small group leaders, or any other failure at implementing a small group structure, this appendix may have the key.

For More Information Read:
• Appendix 3.A: "Errors Regarding Small Groups (and the Cure)"

LARGE AND SMALL GROUPS ARE NEEDED

Large gatherings have the clout and witnesses to create an area-wide or demographic-wide impact. And a large church has greater survivability because it has more resources to draw on.[29] Still, earlier we saw that small groups are the venues in which spiritual questioning, accountability, intimacy, and spiritual growth take place, both in biblical times and today. Let's look at figure 3.1 to see why small and large gatherings are both needed.

Figure 3.1: *Strengths of Small and Large Church Groups*	
Small groups of four to twenty people can:	*Groups of twenty-one or more people can:*
Cultivate intimacy • A person can raise questions that might bring ridicule among those who don't know the person well. • A person can feel one is known as a whole person, and thus one's problems are put in perspective.	Cultivate anonymity • People can learn about delicate topics without having to reveal their own opinions or doubts. • People can anonymously explore a church to see if it is right for them.
Cultivate acceptance of struggles • Religious doubts can be discussed. • Personal problems can be shared.	Cultivate perception of agreement • Power is apparent in unity. • Influence is a byproduct of size.
Cultivate personal impact • Counsel can be customized for personal difficulties. • Because counsel is customized, it may be taken more seriously. • Accountability is strong, because intimacy fosters observation.	Cultivate community impact • Moralizing on community or cultural problems will get noticed. • A large church can be a moral compass for a community.[30]
Cultivate interpersonal commitment • Because members see the benefits, they are staunchly loyal to their small groups. • They will give their time, talents, and treasures if their groups think something is a good idea.	Cultivate organizational commitment • Because members see the needs of the organization, they are moderately loyal to the church. • They will give their time, talents, and treasures if the church leader can convince them it is a good idea.

continued

Figure 3.1: *Strengths of Small and Large Church Groups* continued

Small groups of four to twenty people can:	Groups of twenty-one or more people can:
Cultivate volunteers • Needs are basic and local, so that everyone helps out, leading to expansion of volunteerism. • Novices are given a chance to volunteer under the direct oversight of the group.	Cultivate professionals • Needs are more sophisticated, and professionals are hired. • Experienced volunteers are preferred over novices, resulting in leaders with longer histories of experience.
Cultivate local ministry • Small groups can custom-tailor ministry to their local context, offering specialized ministry in local neighborhoods. • Small groups can stay connected to those they serve over a longer period of time.	Cultivate area- or demographic-wide ministry • The large church can meet sizable community or demographic needs, such as the needs of large groups of immigrants. • A sizable church can be mobilized for disaster relief, etc., and make a bigger impact.
Cultivate low-cost experimentation • Small groups can easily experiment, changing their approach often and quickly. • Small groups can create alternatives that are low-cost and volunteer-driven.	Cultivate proficiency • Large groups can put the money and person power behind ideas and make them better. • Large groups can promote, publish, and distribute information about their ideas.

WHY SMALL IS IMPORTANT

Based on figure 3.1, which is needed—small or large?[31] Both! But I believe the advantages of small (in the left column) remind us that healthy small groups are a critical organizational feature of any size church that wants to fulfill the Great Commission and make disciples. And for influence and survivability, I hope many small churches will become larger, while retaining a healthy, growing smallness via their small groups. And I hope large churches will get smaller too, not in size but in emphasis. Such congregations are uncommon churches, fostering the advantages of both columns in figure 3.1.

A CAVEAT

There is a caveat here. I have found that if you don't make small groups your focus, then showiness, razzle-dazzle, and flashy bigness will overshadow the intimacy and companionship that the less flashy small groups provide. Unfortunately, many growing churches over time focus less on their small groups and become large churches with weak small group infrastructures.[32] And so, unless a church works hard at emphasizing its small groups more than it emphasizes its bigness, the church will lapse into a big-group emphasis and small groups will be sidetracked as just another program.

Thus, because both large and small groups are needed (but small groups may be needed more), are you small enough? By this I mean, do your congregants see your church as primarily focused on small groups, or do the big group gatherings command the most attention? If your answer is the latter (the focus and energy of your church is primarily on church events), then you need to "get small."

HOW TO GET SMALL

It starts by asking yourselves, "Are we are small enough?" As I noted above, I'm not talking about just being a small congregation. I'm talking about any size church that has at its core a healthy network of small, intimate, mutually accountable fellowship groups. Figure 3.2 is a self-test to see if your church is small enough.

You may have found that you are small enough. But most churches find they are not. Anytime there is a significant group of congregants who are not yet connected to a small, mutually supportive fellowship group, your church is not small enough. Now that we've looked at the why for small, let's go to chapter 4 and read about the how.

Figure 3.2: *Are You Small Enough?* (Check all that apply)	
Small Enough	Too Big
☐ We have a staff person in charge of small groups.	☐ The planning for weekend services takes over 20 percent of the staff's weekly time.
☐ Our Sunday school and/or small group attendance is more than 50 percent of your weekend worship attendance.[33]	☐ Fifty percent or more of our paid staff has their primarily responsibly at weekend services.
☐ Our small groups regularly go outside their group setting to serve others.	☐ People in our community know our church primarily for its worship, preaching, or facility.[34]
☐ People in our community know our church primarily for its small groups.	☐ Twenty percent of our attendees seem to do eighty percent of the work.
☐ The largest group of volunteers in our church is our small group leader.	☐ The friends of people in our church primarily sit around them in the worship services.
☐ When people talk about why they attend our church, they usually mention their small group (Sunday school, Bible study, or other group).	☐ When people talk about why they were attracted to our church, they primarily mention the worship, the preaching, a program, the staff, or the facility.
☐ When asked what they do at the church, most people say, "I support it through my small group."	☐ When asked what they do at the church, most people say, "I support it with my prayers and attendance."
☐ Spiritual growth is a primary focus of our church.	☐ Church finances are a worrisome issue at our church.
☐ When something needs to be communicated, the leadership team tells the small group supervisors, who in turn tell the small group leaders who then inform the small groups.	☐ Communication in our church is an ongoing problem.
☐ Newcomers often say they started attending a small group regularly, before they started attending the church worship services regularly.	☐ A lot of newcomers seem to leave the church about eighteen months after their first visit.
Total: _____	Total: _____
If the left column has the most checkmarks, it may indicate your church is small enough.	

HOW DOES A CHURCH GROW S.M.A.L.L.? | 4

For those who skipped directly to this chapter, in chapter 3 we learned that small groups:

1. Are the biblical environment where spiritual growth takes place;

2. Are the historical environment where spiritual growth takes place;

3. Are needed along with large groups;

4. Are easily eclipsed by bigness;

5. Need to be the focal point if you are to create balance; and

6. Foster intimacy, connectivity, and accountability, which have more impact upon making disciples than bigness.[1]

Growing smaller means ushering a church into a new, central focus on small groups that are not cliquish but reach out to those inside and outside of a group. So how is this accomplished? The answer is in five cures, where the first letter of each cure spells S.M.A.L.L.

WEDNESDAY NIGHT SUNDAY SCHOOLS

It had been only six months since Larry had taken over the senior pastor role at Eastlake Church. He had come from several successful pastorates where he planted thriving churches, so few people expected any problems when he took on this large suburban church of six hundred in worship attendance. But I had sensed a potential for conflict and was not completely taken aback when I received a late night call from Larry.

"Bob, you've got to fly down here this weekend," Larry began with a note of urgency.

"That's short notice," I replied.

"Well, if you don't, I won't be here much longer," continued Larry. "The board has called for a vote of confidence. This has never happened to me in the churches I planted. If you can come down here and help me sort this out, I think I can survive their vote."

And survive Larry did. However, it was not easy. What I found when I arrived at Eastlake Church was that the leaders were upset over the new small group program that Pastor Larry had begun to implement.

"At the churches I planted, they liked the small groups we had on Sunday night," recalled Larry. "People got connected to each other and a lot of growth took place in those Sunday evening Life Groups. Some met at the church, some in homes, and some at other times during the week. That is how we grew, and that is why Eastlake leaders wanted me here."

And Larry was right. The churches he planted had grown remarkably fast because of a central emphasis upon discipleship in small groups. And now Larry brought this passion for Sunday evening small groups to Eastlake. From the pulpit, Larry had weekly extolled the virtues of small Sunday evening groups, admonishing everyone to attend one. The plan of getting people into small groups was laudable; the execution was not.

For almost fifty years, adult Sunday schools had been Eastlake's focus. "When Larry arrived we had about seven hundred adults in Sunday schools and six hundred adults in worship," remembered a board member. This is not uncommon in Baptist churches where Sunday school attendance often outpaces worship attendance. Subsequently, most Eastlake attendees had their small groups; they just called them Sunday schools.

Larry however, had planted several youthful churches. "Because the under-thirty crowd have Sunday evenings free, we got everyone into Sunday evening small groups," Larry recalled. So when he came to Eastlake, he tried the same strategy there. "I see now how I blew it," stated Larry. "I told Eastlake congregants they must come back Sunday evening and be part of our Life Groups, or they weren't going to grow in Christ. I see why they got angry. I didn't realize they already had small groups in their Sunday schools."

"So why not call your Sunday evening Life Groups 'Sunday evening Sunday schools?'" I suggested. "This church sees the power of small groups in their adult Sunday school experience. Usually in this circumstance, they can see the value of Sunday schools at other times, especially for people who can't make it on Sunday mornings."

Larry followed this advice and added some creative elements of his own. Soon, in addition to a Sunday evening Sunday school, Eastlake had a Wednesday evening Sunday school. The names seemed a bit awkward, but the congregation did not seem to mind. The Sunday school program created community and intimacy in this large congregation. Within eighteen months, Eastlake had more than nine hundred adults attending one of its three Sunday school options.

As a result, Larry discovered that small groups already existed at Eastlake. "I'm glad I stuck with an emphasis on small groups," recalled Larry. "But we built on the foundation of small groups the church already had."

℞2 FOR THE COMMON CHURCH = GROW S.M.A.L.L.

In this cure, as well as in all of the cures in this book, the prescriptions spell out the name of the cure. Here the cure is S.M.A.L.L., where each letter represents:

- **CURE S:** Survey your small groups.
- **CURE M:** Missionalize all small groups.
- **CURE A:** Add more small groups.
- **CURE L:** Lead small groups.
- **CURE L:** Locate your focus in small groups.

CURE S = SURVEY YOUR SMALL GROUPS

A Comprehensive Definition of Small Groups

There are many ways to define a small group. When you ask most people, they will identify a small group as a home fellowship group like those made popular by the small group movement and exemplified by the body-life churches, vineyard churches, and alpha groups.[2]

But small groups in churches are more than just home-fellowship groups, because any small group of individuals that is meeting semi-regularly and growing in closeness is technically a small group. Therefore, *all* of the following church groups are types of small groups:

- Sunday school classes;
- classes of any type (Bible, topical, and twelve-step programs);
- standing leadership committees;
- task groups (worship, program, project, ministry, and facility upkeep); and
- fellowship groups (home groups, Bible studies, lunch groups, alpha groups, and sports teams).

Therefore, to grow small, let's begin with figure 4.1, a broad definition that ensures you don't overlook any of the small groups you have already.

With such a comprehensive definition, you can see that you already have many small groups in your church. The key is to first survey them, and then to apply the remaining cures in this chapter to help them refocus on a biblical purpose.

Figure 4.1: *A Comprehensive Definition of a Small Group*

Any regular gathering within a church's fellowship network, meeting more than one time a month with typically less than twenty attendees.[3]

Survey All Small Groups

Now that we have a working definition of small groups, the next step is to use this definition to count them. Be careful not to miss any, because if you do, you cannot help them refocus on their purpose. Figure 4.2 will help you total them. But if you have some small groups that have grown too large (twenty or more people), it may be necessary to divide them into several small groups. See appendix 4.A for ideas about how to create new

For More Information Read:
- Appendix 4.A: "Are Some Small Groups Too Big? Don't Divide, Compartmentalize!"

smaller groups within groups that have grown too big for intimacy and accountability.

Now use your definition above with figure 4.2 to count your small groups. Keep these guidelines in mind:

- Count only adult small groups at this time (teenage and above). While children need small groups such as Sunday schools, this chart will look at how to expand and refocus your adult groups.
- List your small groups under the type of group that best describes them. And even though some groups could fit under several different types of small groups (for example, an adult Sunday school class could also be a task group), list each small group only under one type of small group. It is not as important that each group fits into the ideal category as that all groups are listed in figure 4.2 (use additional rows as needed).

Figure 4.2: *Survey Your Small Groups*	
Name of small group	*Average size*
Adult Sunday Schools and Other Classes	
1.	
2.	
3.	
4.	
5. *(Use additional pages as needed)*	
Standing Committees	
6.	
7.	
8.	
9.	
10. *(Use additional pages as needed)*	*continued*

Figure 4.2: *Survey Your Small Groups* continued	
Name of small group	Average size
Task Groups (worship, program, project, ministry, facility upkeep)	
11.	
12.	
13.	
14.	
15. *(Use additional pages as needed)*	
Fellowship Groups (home groups, Bible studies, lunch groups, alpha groups, sports teams) 16.	
17.	
18.	
19.	
20. *(Use additional pages as needed)*	
Prayer Groups	
21.	
22.	
23.	
24.	
25. *(Use additional pages as needed)*	

Are you surprised? Most churches are amazed by how many small groups they already have. But as noted in the story of Eastlake Church, this is why congregants often resist small group programs. When people are already attending an informal small group, such as a Bible study, Sunday school, committee, or sports team, they will often resist the idea of joining another small group.

Publicly Recognize All Small Groups

After surveying your small groups, publicly acknowledge that all of these groups are small groups. People who already attend a small group will be less likely to balk at launching a small group program, because they understand their small group is already part of it.

Once you know where your small groups are and how they are already teeming within your church, it's time to move to the next part of the prescription: to missionalize them.

CURE M = MISSIONALIZE ALL SMALL GROUPS

What Is This Talk about Missional?

The term *missional* is a recent expression that describes a church where everyone is involved in reaching out to non-churchgoers and churchgoers in order to better reconnect everyone to their loving heavenly Father. Some have found eight patterns of a missional church, stating that a missional church:[4]

1. Sees outreach to non-churchgoers as the responsibility of every person in the church (not just a committee or the staff).

2. Is based upon biblical principles.

3. Takes risks to help the needy.

4. Lives in a loving and forgiving way that points the community toward a relationship with God and personal conversion.

5. Worships in way that even non-churchgoers sense God's presence.

6. Depends on the Holy Spirit through prayer and anointing.

7. Points others toward reconnecting with a loving, heavenly Father, not toward people, buildings, or programs.

8. Works together in harmony, though with different duties.

These are missional patterns that almost any church would want to embrace. But many people first react negatively toward the term *missional* because it is new, and they do not fully know its meaning. But the eight patterns of missional faithfulness are good behaviors to strive for. And so, the term *missional* is helpful. I have defined it this way: A missional church seeks to work together with the Holy Spirit to convey the good news that our heavenly Father wants to restore fellowship with his wayward offspring.

Missionalizing Small Groups

A triangle can be a useful symbol to depict the three types of growth that every small group must experience if it is to fulfill the eight patterns.[5] Missional small groups must be:

Growing UP— This means a small group is growing in its connection to God through prayer, Bible study, and the prophetic ministry of mature leaders. The group is connecting upward to God, and he is responding with power, passion, and purpose.

Growing IN— This indicates a small group is serving existing Christians and growing closer together by praying for one another, encouraging one another, and meeting one another's needs. Examples can include spiritually serving people inside the church (such as praying for them) or administratively serving people inside the church (such as committee work).

Growing OUT— This reminds a small group that it must always be growing in its service to non-churchgoers.

Figure 4.3 is a triangle with one leg leading outward. This variation reminds us that a healthy small group has three inter-reliant functions that operate concurrently and that this includes an outward focus too.

Figure 4.3:
Missionalize Small Groups by Requiring UP-IN-OUT Ministry

UP-IN-OUT Balance

The problem is that many small groups only focus on one or two of the arrows and not all three. The result is imbalance. For instance, church committees can spend an unbalanced amount of time on IN tasks such as committee work, administration, and organization directed toward meeting the needs of churchgoers. Such tasks are important if the administrative duties of the church are to be accomplished. Yet, all IN work without corresponding UP (heavenward) and OUT (serving others outside the church) work will result in a committee that is inward looking, burned out, and focused on only meeting the needs of those inside the congregation.

So the cure for the common church is to have its small groups equally growing in all three areas. To balance these three areas is what I call "missionalizing a small group," or in other words, groups that understand their participation in God's mission involves three duties:

- UP-ward connection,
- IN-ward ministry, and
- OUT-ward service.

Therefore, to missionalize your small groups and make them uncommonly healthy, you must analyze how well each group is addressing UP-IN-OUT. Then brainstorm improvements that can bring all three areas into balance. Use figure 4.4 as an evaluation template. Make one for each small group.

Figure 4.4: *Small Group Evaluation—Creating Missional Balance*			
(TEMPLATE: create this figure for each small group)			
A.	B.	C.	D.
Small group name:	What is it doing to grow in each area?	Which area(s) is (are) weak?	What should be done to improve weak area(s), and when will this take place?
	UP IN OUT		

To conduct your evaluation (figure 4.4) of each small group, do the following:

1. Fill out figure 4.4 for each small group.

2. Meet with the leaders of each group and ask for their input. Add this to figure 4.4.

3. The small group leader and church leaders should agree on column D.

4. Use the mutually agreed upon column D to check progress in ninety days.

CURE A = ADD MORE SMALL GROUPS

Over the years, there have been several ways to count how many small groups a church needs. Most have suggested that between 60 and 75 percent of a congregation's churchgoers should be involved in small groups.[6] After years of consulting and helping churches missionalize their small groups, let me suggest the following ratios.

Figure 4.5: Percentage of Weekend Worship Attendance Involved in Small Groups	
Healthy church:	More than 60 percent involved in a small group of some kind.
Marginal church:	20–59 percent involved in a small group of some kind.
Ailing church:	Less than 20 percent involved in a small group of some kind.

Look at figure 4.6, and brainstorm with small group leaders where more small groups can be added.

Figure 4.6: Adding More Small Groups		
Name of small group	Potential Size	Who will lead it? How often will it meet? Who will oversee it?
Adult Sunday Schools		
1.		
2.		
3.		
4.		
5. (Use additional pages as needed)		
Standing Committees		
6.		
7.		
8.		
9.		
10. (Use additional pages as needed)		
Task Groups (worship, program, project, ministry, facility upkeep)		
11.		
12.		
13.		
14.		
15. (Use additional pages as needed)		continued

Figure 4.6: *Adding More Small Groups* *continued*

Name of small group	Potential Size	Who will lead it? How often will it meet? Who will oversee it?
Fellowship Groups (home groups, Bible studies, lunch groups, alpha groups, sports teams)		
16.		
17.		
18.		
19.		
20. *(Use additional pages as needed)*		
Prayer Groups		
21.		
22.		
23.		
24.		
25. *(Use additional pages as needed)*		
	Increase =	

How to add small groups:

1. Total the middle column (the potential sizes of all additional small groups).

2. Add this increase to the total number of attendees in small groups from figure 4.2.

3. Compare this new small group attendance number with the number of attendees you need to add to move to the next level of small groups (in other words, from an ailing church to a marginal church, or from a marginal church to a healthy church).

4. Distribute this list to department heads and leaders who might be potential small group leaders or supervisors. It is important that you do not have any small groups that are lacking some sort of oversight. This is necessary to promote unity, leadership development, and discipleship of the small group leaders.

5. Agree with the person who will lead or supervise each group what progress will be made toward starting the group over the next ninety days.

6. Check back in ninety days.

7. Redraft figure 4.6 as needed, tracking small groups that are successfully launched.

Once you have created a plan to add more small groups, you must delve deeper into the leadership of these groups. It is mature and effective leadership that will be key to maintaining healthy small groups.

CUR͟E L = LEAD SMALL GROUPS

While most small groups will have a leader, the leadership that is needed to oversee a network of small groups is often marginal if not missing. For small groups to maintain cohesiveness, two types of leaders are required: (1) small group leaders; and (2) supervisors who will mentor small group leaders; while linking small groups together and to the organization.

Small Group Supervisors

Let's look at the importance of small group supervisors first.[7] Here are the six elements of effective small group oversight:[8]

1. The small group supervisor does exactly what the name says: gives oversight, counsel, and mentorship to small group leaders.

2. The supervisor does not supervise individual members of the group, but rather mentors the leaders of the small groups.[9]

3. The small group supervisor provides leadership training and development for the small group leaders under her or his care.[10]

4. The oversight process is depicted visually, such as in a flow chart. Too often small group leaders have only a vague idea of who they report to and how other small groups relate to theirs.

5. Each supervisor oversees not more than ten small group leaders. Many small group strategies fail because one person tries to oversee a myriad of groups. Jesus gave us the example of discipling twelve (Luke 6:12–16). And Jethro, Moses' father-in-law, reminded Moses that he should give direct oversight to only ten people (Ex. 18:13–27).

6. Taking into consideration Jethro's principle means that a church that has more than ten groups (and as we saw in figure 4.2, you probably do) will need a supervisor over the supervisors. This supervisor of supervisors is often a staff-level small groups pastor or discipleship pastor[11] who directly oversees supervisors of small group leaders. St. Thomas' Church in Sheffield, England, calls a grouping of ten small groups a cluster. The leader over ten small groups is a cluster leader, and a leader over ten cluster leaders is called a lay pastor.

Small Group Leaders Must Set the UP-IN-OUT Agenda

Usually small group leaders have a lot to do at a small group meeting, but if care is not taken to address all three elements of a healthy small group (UP-IN-OUT), then one or more of the elements will get overlooked. To combat the tendency to overlook one or more of the UP-IN-OUT elements, the first thirty minutes of every small group should include ten minutes each of UP, IN, and OUT reflection. This emphasis is preserved by two elements:

1. Put a standing item on the agenda for every group that the first thirty minutes of every meeting will include the UP-IN-OUT reflection. See figure 4.2 for an example.

2. Use some of the discussion starters (questions) from figure 6.3 (in chapter 6) to draw out UP-IN-OUT reflection.

Small Groups Can Divide Their UP-IN-OUT Responsibilities

As we saw above, most small groups gravitate toward one or two elements of UP-IN-OUT. To combat this, some churches will utilize three (volunteer) leaders in every small group:

- An UP leader helps the group focus on connection with God in every meeting. This often may be a worship leader.
- An IN leader helps the group focus on one another's needs. This often is a prayer-oriented person.
- An OUT leader is one of the most important leaders of such a group. It has been my experience that if an UP leader and an IN leader are not available, an OUT leader can help keep a small group connected UP and IN by focusing on the needs of those outside the congregation. I contend that if you have only one of the three leaders in a small group, the OUT leader is the most important.

While this is beyond the volunteer power of smaller churches, if you have a strong small group system, appendix 4.B describes how to utilize UP, IN, and OUT leaders in every small group within a church.

Once a church has surveyed its small groups, missionalized them, added more groups, and is leading them with supervisors and an UP-IN-OUT emphasis, the church must move on to the last phase: locating the focus of your church in discipleship through small groups.

TAKE A LOOK

For More Information Read:
- Appendix 4.B: "Leading Small Groups with Three Leaders: UP Leaders, IN Leaders, and OUT Leaders"

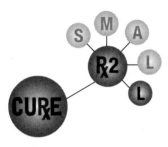

CURE L = LOCATE YOUR FOCUS IN SMALL GROUPS

Locate Small Groups as an Element of Mission and Vision Statements

Since large gatherings can create excitement and attention, they often overshadow the key discipleship venue of small groups. To combat this, leaders must ensure that the church's emphasis on small groups is highlighted noticeably in official statements.

One of the most important places to highlight your small group focus is in a church's mission, vision, and personality statements.[12] These statements usually include many central and worthwhile characteristics of a church. But if a church is going to disciple people, then small groups are going to be a primary focus, and this emphasis must be highlighted in all three statements.

Locate Newcomer Connection in Small Groups

Churches often have programs to reach out to newcomers. Yet I have observed that the most successful programs focus on getting newcomers into small groups.[13]

Too often churches laud features such as their impressive facilities, music, and children's programs in their newcomer literature and orientations. But really, newcomers are looking to connect with people like themselves, people among whom they can be authentic and open, sharing spiritual hurts and questions. Therefore, newcomer ministries should seek to connect newcomers to a small group where these needs can be best addressed with intimacy and adaptation.

But because existing small groups can quickly become closed (or at least cold)[14] to outsiders, the best tactic is to start new groups for newcomers as soon as possible. In very small congregations, a newcomers' small group can be publicized and then started once there are four or more newcomers showing interest.

If a newcomer ministry does not have the connection of newcomers to a small group as its central focus, then at best those newcomers will become an audience, and at worst they will leave the church. Remember, Thom Rainer found, "New Christians who immediately became active [in a small group are] five times more likely to remain in the church five years later than those who were active in worship services alone."[15]

The best approach is to locate small groups as the central focus of your newcomer ministry by three actions:

1. Start new small groups comprised of newcomers if you have a sufficient newcomer flow. Large churches (over five hundred in adult weekend worship) can usually start a newcomers' group every month. Larger churches can start them more frequently, smaller ones less so. The key is to offer a newcomer small group as soon as you have more than four newcomers interested (not counting small group leaders).

2. Provide a clear, convenient path into a newcomer's small group. Try to have the newcomers' small group as closely associated in time and location to their visit time and location. For instance, if newcomers primarily visit on Sunday mornings, then offer a Sunday morning newcomers' small group during your Sunday school hour. Remember, the more distant in time and location your newcomers' small group is to the time and location of their visit, the less likely newcomers are to attend.

3. Promote small groups in all of your newcomer literature, publicity, and gatherings.

Locate Sermon Teaching in Small Groups

A final aspect of locating small groups at the center of a congregation's life is to disseminate sermon lessons through your small groups. Larry Osborne, pastor of North Coast Community Church in Vista, California, has been an innovator in sermon-based small groups.[16] His key is to provide all small groups with questions for study based on the previous week's sermon. This accomplishes three things:

1. Allows congregants who missed the weekend sermon to catch up on what the rest of the church learned.

2. Unites the church because all small groups are hearing the same message. Small groups are less likely to become detached and divisive this way.

3. Allows congregants to explore and apply sermon lessons in a more intimate, ask-assertive, localized way.

Church leaders who want to locate sermon lessons as a unifying and local element of small groups must undertake the following four elements:

1. Preachers must write questions for group discussion at the same time they write their sermon, providing copies to the small group supervisors.

2. Small group supervisors must oversee the distribution (usually electronically) of the questions to all small group leaders.

3. Depending on what the topic of the sermon is, the person in charge of moderating the discussion of the questions can be either the small group's UP, IN, or OUT leader.

4. The supervisors use the sermon topic and questions as starting places to maintain dialogue and mentor small group leaders.

"But," you may ask, "what if some of our small groups such as boards, sport teams, and music groups do not have a teaching time? How can they locate the sermon in the center of their small group?" The key is for every small group, regardless of function, to be required to have a discussion or teaching time with questions. This location of the sermon message at the core of all small groups can expand the unity and biblical focus of a church.

CONCLUSION

Getting small is critical today. And though there has been a lot written about small groups, because many programs do not have the S.M.A.L.L. elements, they can be inadequate. Follow the S.M.A.L.L. approach, where the R_X2 for the common church is to grow S.M.A.L.L. with the following structure:

- **CURE S:** Survey your small groups.
- **CURE M:** Missionalize all small groups.
- **CURE A:** Add more small groups.
- **CURE L:** Lead small groups.
- **CURE L:** Locate your focus in small groups.

QUESTIONS FOR GROUP AND PERSONAL REFLECTION

CURE S = SURVEY YOUR SMALL GROUPS

Question 1: In which categories (of figure 4.2) do you feel your church should have more small groups and how many?

Prior to answering this question, fill out figure 4.2. Discuss your response with others.

CURE M = MISSIONALIZE ALL SMALL GROUPS

Question 2: How many of your small groups are unbalanced between UP-IN-OUT ministry?

Prior to answering this question, use figure 4.4 to evaluate all small groups in which you participate or to which you give oversight. Then rank them with those at the top being more balanced and those at the bottom with less balance between UP-IN-OUT ministry. Answer the following questions:

- Which groups are the most balanced? What can other groups learn from them?
- Which groups are the most important to the effective running of the church's organizational structure? How balanced or unbalanced are they?
- What will you do over the next ninety days to correct the issues identified in question 2 above?

CURE A = ADD MORE SMALL GROUPS

Question 3: According to figure 4.6, what groups should you add, and how will you do it?

Meet with other leaders to pool your answers from figure 4.6. Then undertake the following:

1. Total the middle column (the potential sizes of all additional small groups).

2. Add this increase to the total number of attendees in small groups from figure 4.2.

3. Compare this new small group attendance number with the number of attendees you need to add to move to the next level of small groups (for example, from an ailing church to a marginal church, or from a marginal church to a healthy church).

4. Distribute this list to department heads and leaders who might be potential small group leaders or supervisors. It is important that you do not have any small groups that do not have some sort of oversight. This is necessary to promote unity, leadership development, and discipleship of the small group leaders.

5. Agree with the person who will lead or supervise each group what progress will be made toward starting the group over the next ninety days.

6. Plan a date to check back in ninety days on progress.

7. Redraft figure 4.6 as needed, tracking small groups that are successfully launched.

CURE L = LEAD SMALL GROUPS

Question 4: Does your church emphasize UP-IN-OUT in every small group, and do you have supervisors over all small groups? If not, what will you suggest be done?

Chart or graph the small group network you perceive in the church. Share your charts with other leaders, gaining their input and creating an agreed-upon master chart. Note deficiencies, gaps, and where supervisors are needed. Also note if these groups are incorporating an agenda that includes reflection on UP-IN-OUT elements. Discuss how this can be addressed.

CURE L = LOCATE YOUR FOCUS IN SMALL GROUPS

Question 4: Pick the most pressing questions from the following to address:

- Are small groups an integral part of your church's mission, vision, and personality statements? Why or why not? What do you suggest be done?
- Are small groups effectively connecting newcomers to your church? Why or why not? What do you suggest be done?
- Are sermon teachings an integral part of your small groups? Why or why not? What do you suggest be done?

Locating the focus of a church's vision, newcomer connections, and teaching in small groups is a characteristic of healthy and growing churches.[17] Discuss where your church is deficient in these areas, and describe concrete plans you will undertake to address this and evaluate progress.

GROW L.E.A.R.N.ers

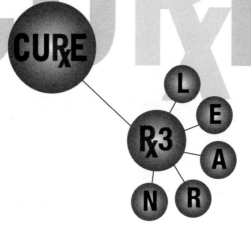

WHY GROW L.E.A.R.N.ERS? | 5

"Yours may be a COMMON CHURCH if your primary goal(s) is (are) . . ."
(SELF-SCORING—Check all that apply)

☐ To have better worship services.

☐ To survive as a church.

☐ To be a church that goes out into the community to serve.

☐ To baptize new converts.

☐ To turn around a declining church.

☐ To be a close-knit community of believers.

☐ To have high quality programming and ministry.

☐ To implement church change.

☐ To preserve a church's legacy.

☐ To be known as a church with exceptional teaching.

WHAT IS THE GOAL OF A CHURCH?

I often ask my client churches to tell me what they perceive as their church's primary goal. This is not a scientific poll because these churches need to grow, and they realize this (or they wouldn't be hiring a church growth consultant). But their answers may mirror yours. Look at their responses in figure 5.1.

Figure 5.1: Question to Clients: "What do you perceive as your church's primary goal?"	
To survive as a church.	38 percent
To provide a warm and caring fellowship.	22 percent
To win souls to Christ.	21 percent
To influence community morals for the better.	11 percent
None of the above.	8 percent

As you can see from figure 5.1, the common answer is to survive as a church. This desire to survive is laudable, and such honesty is encouraging. Yet, with survival as a primary goal, a church usually won't continue to exist much longer. This cure for the common church is much bigger, for it is a church-wide refocus back to Jesus' goal for his church.

Jesus' Goal for the Church

The right answer for figure 5.1 is actually "none of the above" and comes from Jesus' own words. That's right, the primary goal of every church is not to influence the community for the better, provide a warm place of fellowship, sponsor excellent teaching, or even survive. The church of God has a higher, more encompassing call (that, by the way, includes the previous tasks).[1] To understand this, let's look at Jesus' last and most poignant instructions to his followers (figure 5.2, the Great Commission).

Figure 5.2: *Jesus' Great Commission (Matt. 28:18–20 CEB)*
(commissioning verbs are underlined)

Jesus came near and spoke to them, "I've received all authority in heaven and on earth. Therefore, go and make disciples of all nations, baptizing them in the name of the Father and of the Son and of the Holy Spirit, teaching them to obey everything that I've commanded you. Look, I myself will be with you every day until the end of this present age."

What Makes This a Great Commission?[2]

The Great Commission is the label that has been given to these final and central instructions Jesus gave his followers in Matthew 28:19–20. In this paragraph, Jesus literally commissioned or recruited all followers down through the ages into his mission. This commissioning is akin to an official directive, a direct order, and a command, such as a military conscript might receive upon entering service. In fact, military personnel reading this will no doubt remember their own commissioning into the armed forces. Veterans have told me this was a powerful and moving experience, with one veteran stating, "You weren't supposed to have tears in your eyes when you were commissioned, but I did. After 9/11 it was clear to me that I was no longer talking about serving my country. I was doing it! I was ready to put my life on the line for my country."

Christians too are called to put their lives on the line in Jesus' great commissioning. Here is what others have said about this passage (figure 5.3):

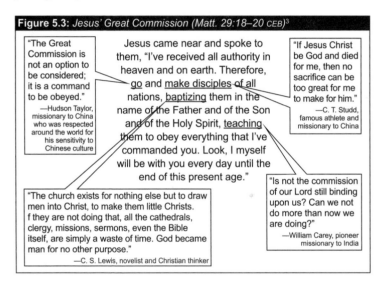

Figure 5.3: *Jesus' Great Commission (Matt. 29:18–20 CEB)*[3]

"The Great Commission is not an option to be considered; it is a command to be obeyed."
—Hudson Taylor, missionary to China who was respected around the world for his sensitivity to Chinese culture

Jesus came near and spoke to them, "I've received all authority in heaven and on earth. Therefore, go and make disciples of all nations, baptizing them in the name of the Father and of the Son and of the Holy Spirit, teaching them to obey everything that I've commanded you. Look, I myself will be with you every day until the end of this present age."

"If Jesus Christ be God and died for me, then no sacrifice can be too great for me to make for him."
—C. T. Studd, famous athlete and missionary to China

"The church exists for nothing else but to draw men into Christ, to make them little Christs. f they are not doing that, all the cathedrals, clergy, missions, sermons, even the Bible itself, are simply a waste of time. God became man for no other purpose."
—C. S. Lewis, novelist and Christian thinker

"Is not the commission of our Lord still binding upon us? Can we not do more than now we are doing?"
—William Carey, pioneer missionary to India

THE FOUR VERBS OF JESUS' GREAT COMMISSION

Because this Great Commission is so important, it is not surprising that each word, each phrase that Jesus uttered in Matthew 28:19–20, seems to have been chosen carefully to convey his message. Jesus undoubtedly knew that believers through history would return to this passage as they contemplated the goal of their spiritual community.

Jesus used four commissioning verbs in this commission. Because the Greek language (in which much of the New Testament was written) is much more precise than today's English, Jesus was able to use a special wording that stressed one verb as the primary verb over the other three. In figure 5.4, let's look closer at the verbs in his Great Commission and see if we can locate the one that Jesus emphasized as its central aim.

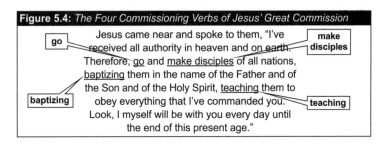

Figure 5.4: *The Four Commissioning Verbs of Jesus' Great Commission*

Jesus came near and spoke to them, "I've received all authority in heaven and on earth. Therefore, go and make disciples of all nations, baptizing them in the name of the Father and of the Son and of the Holy Spirit, teaching them to obey everything that I've commanded you. Look, I myself will be with you every day until the end of this present age."

go — make disciples — baptizing — teaching

Finding the Main Verb

In English, the four verbs seem equal. But when Jesus spoke these words, he pronounced one verb with a special spelling, thereby indicating that this verb was the main verb or goal of the passage. Which verb was Jesus pointing to as the goal of his Great Commission?

Take Away the Three Helping Verbs to Find the Main Verb

You are probably thinking, "What are the other verbs?" The three other verbs are called participles, which means they are helping verbs that tell how the main verb will be accomplished.[4] Jesus chose specific spellings to show that three verbs are participles telling you how to accomplish the main verb.[5]

So which three verbs are participles (telling us how) and which one verb is the main verb (telling us the goal)? The spelling of the Greek verbs indicates the following.[6]

Go is a participle, and it tells us how we fulfill the Great Commission, in other words by "going" and "as we are going."

Make disciples is the Greek word *matheteusate* and is the main verb. Because Jesus pronounced "make disciples" with a special spelling, he made it clear to his Greek hearers that, "Your goal is to make disciples, and how you make them is by going, baptizing, and teaching." Now that we've discovered the main verb, let's look briefly at the two remaining participles.

Baptizing is important in distinguishing how to make disciples, for it reminds us that baptism is a personal, public, and supernatural acknowledgment of new birth in Christ.

Teaching reminds us that a key aspect of the how of disciple making is teaching them about their loving Father. Sometimes I find people who think teaching is the goal, but teaching is really just the process. We teach to make learners.

Therefore, the uncommon church's goal must not be the going, the baptizing, or even the teaching. These are the hows. In the words Jesus chose, he made clear that for the uncommon church he was founding, "making disciples" was the goal.

WHAT DO DISCIPLES LOOK LIKE?

As a junior high student, I heard a pastor say we are to make disciples. Being an inattentive youth, I never quite grasped a correct image of what this looked like. From my rudimentary knowledge of the Bible, I pictured Jesus' disciples and figured the church should make more long-haired individuals with beards, robes, and sandals. Because the only image I could conjure were the hippies of the era, I wondered in my naïveté, "Was the preacher really telling us to go out and produce more hippies?" Obviously this is not what the preacher intended. But the word *disciple* had become so archaic and disconnected that a modern depiction was needed.

Picturing a Disciple

To picture a disciple, we begin with the Greek word *math-eteusate*, which means "a learner, a pupil or an apprentice."[7] Rather than an expert, it carries the image of a trainee or a student. Christ was commanding his followers not to produce experts, but rather to foster a community of authentic learners. Following Jesus should feel like you are enrolled in his school of learning. Therefore, a church is not a cadre of experts, but a college of fellow learners.

Theologians have sought to convey the rich and multifaceted meaning of the verb *to make disciples* in several ways:

- Donald McGavran: "It means enroll in [Jesus'] school."[8]
- Eddie Gibbs: "It is learning, not simply through being given information, but in learning how to use it. Discipleship is an apprenticeship rather than an academic way of learning. It is learning by doing."[9]
- James Engel: "In short, discipleship requires continued obedience over time. . . . Thus becoming a disciple is a *process* beginning when one received Christ, continuing over a lifetime as one is conformed to his image (Phil. 1:6), and culminating in the glory at the end of the age."[10]

An Up-to-Date Image of a Disciple

From a closer look at the words Jesus used, we see that the goal of every church is to help people become "a community of active, ongoing learners."[11] It is not only to baptize or teach as we are going out (though all of these are hows of the disciple-making process). The goal toward which a church should focus its attention and resources is to produce people who are actively learning about their heavenly Father.

Still, this goal includes binding up their wounds, meeting their needs before they even know who Christ is, standing up for justice, and righting wrongs. But all of these worthy actions, if they become the goal, will misguide your mission. God's goal—the purpose he has for every church—is to reconnect his wayward offspring to himself (the essence of the *missio Dei*). And the church's goal (figure 5.5) is to foster this reunification by helping people become learners about a loving, seeking Father.

THE GOAL OF THE CHURCH DEFINED

While the common church has mistaken many hows for the goal, figure 5.5 is the goal against which the uncommon church will be measured. In our commissioning, Jesus has handed us a different measuring stick.

Jesus wants the uncommon church to focus on reuniting his wayward offspring with the Lord by making active,

> **Figure 5.5:** *The Goal of a Church*
> The goal of a church is . . .
> ***To make active, ongoing learners.***
> (learning about a heavenly Father who loves them, sacrificed his Son for them, and who wants to reunite and empower them)

ongoing learners about his great love, sacrifice, and future for them. And so, be careful not to make some of the following common missteps.

Teaching without Learning

If a church is teaching many people, but few are actively learning over a long period of time, the church is not making active, ongoing learners.

Having Learned Once but Not Learning Now

If a church has many people who have learned in the past but are not learning now, then the church is not making active, ongoing learners.

Baptizing without Ongoing Learning

If the church is baptizing many souls, but there is little ongoing education about what it means to follow Christ, then that church is not making active, ongoing learners.

For More Information Read:
• Appendix 5.A: "What the Greek Tells Us about Making Disciples"

In this chapter, we have seen the why of making learners. It's because nurturing learners is the goal of the Great Commission that Christ has given us. In the next chapter, we will learn how to make learners.

HOW DOES A CHURCH | 6
GROW L.E.A.R.N.ers?

In chapter 5, we learned the following about why the uncommon church focuses on growing learners:

- The goal of a church (according to Jesus' Great Commission in Matt. 28:19–20) is to "make disciples."
- An accurate interpretation of this phrase is to make active, ongoing learners.
- Disciples are learning about a heavenly Father who loves them, sacrificed his Son for them, and wants to reunite and empower them.[1]

Churches often mistake going, baptizing, and teaching (the hows) for the goal of making active, ongoing learners.[2] With this in mind, let's look at the hows of making active, ongoing learners.

EILEEN AND BARRY

"I got a lot out of going to church when I was young," began Eileen. "There was a lot of good teaching, and it really seemed to build toward confirmation. I guess that was when I was learning the most, but it all went downhill from there." Eileen had been raised in the stately confines of a Lutheran church amid mysterious, beautiful hymns.

Barry was raised five hundred miles away amid the hand clapping of a Midwest gospel church. "But Eileen and I experienced the same thing," added Barry. "Everything built up to baptism or confirmation. But afterward, when we became teenagers, the teaching emphasis in our churches quickly disappeared."

"Our youth group was more interested in fun, campouts, that sort of stuff," said Eileen. "Those things replaced learning for my friends and me. And as learning disappeared, so did a lot of my spirituality."

"Me too," added Barry. "It wasn't until both of us met Christ in college and went to a church that focused on biblically hungry young people like ourselves that we started to learn again."

"Yes," concluded Eileen, "once we discovered a church where teaching young adults was engaging, relevant, and the focus, we started learning again. And we haven't stopped!"

R3 FOR THE COMMON CHURCH = GROW L.E.A.R.N.ers

If learners are the goal, then let's begin where we left off in chapter 5 with the three how verbs of Matthew 28:19–20. For those who have jumped right to this chapter, we discovered in chapter 5 that Jesus gave three hows for accomplishing the goal of making active, ongoing learners. They are:

- "Go" (v. 19). This verb denotes that you make disciples as you go through daily life and meet the needs of people outside of a church. (Chapters 1 and 2 of this book explain how to do this.)

- "Baptizing" (v. 19). Baptism is a ritual of incorporation into a Christian church, but in Jesus' day, it was more than that. In ancient times, baptisms were held in public spaces where all of the townspeople could observe and attest to the public declaration that a disciple was making. In this chapter, we will look at how to reconnect public declarations with baptism. This lesson will be represented by the first letter of L.E.A.R.N.

- "Teaching" (v. 20). This will be explained via the four remaining letters of L.E.A.R.N

In this cure, as well as in all the cures in this book, the prescription spells out the name of the cure. Here are the letters and their meanings:

For More Information Read:
- Appendix 6.A: "Examples of Commendable Church Goals That Are Not Jesus' Goal"

- **CU℞E L:** Link learners publicly with a community of learners.
- **CU℞E E:** Every small group becomes a learning group.
- **CU℞E A:** Agreement emerges from learning.
- **CU℞E R:** Reproductive learners produce more learners.
- **CU℞E N:** Needs are met through learning-based action.

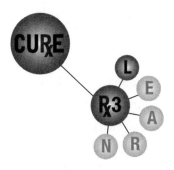

CU℞ₓE L = LINK LEARNERS PUBLICLY WITH A COMMUNITY OF LEARNERS

Why Link Learners Publicly?

Jesus underscored the importance of baptism when he cited it as one of the three hows for fulfilling the Great Commission. To better understand baptism, let's look at how Paul explained it to a largely uninformed Roman audience: "Therefore, we were buried together with him through baptism into his death, so that just as Christ was raised from the dead through the glory of the Father, we too can walk in newness of life" (Rom. 6:4 CEB).

Baptism Creates a Supernatural Connection. Paul explained to his Roman readers that baptism means personally imitating the bodily actions of Jesus. Paul explained this in the first two phrases of Romans 6:4.

Baptism Creates Public Testimony and Public Accountability. The phrase "walk in newness of life" emphasizes the unfolding and visible outcomes that should result after baptism. It is important to remember that in Jesus' day, baptism was a public action that required a new convert go to a public place and demonstrate that he or she now identified with Christ and fellow learners.

Unfortunately, today the public declaration aspect of baptism has been mostly hidden by holding baptism in our sanctuaries. Though many young churches baptize openly (such as Journey

Church in New York City, which baptizes in the chilly Atlantic Ocean), most churches have acquiesced to the comfortable confines of our church auditoriums.

But this robs baptism of its element of public accountability and testimony. The fact that John the Baptist could rebuke detractors among the throngs indicates that many people were in attendance, both those for and against the baptismal action. Such public declaration that links a new believer to Christ, a learning community, and personal change is often missing today.

Two Steps to Linking Learners

Step 1: Link Baptism with Public Testimony and Accountability. The public locations where baptism took place reminded New Testament learners of the open nature of their affiliation with Christ. Today, a public linking with Christ and his community of learners can create accountability from both inside and outside the church. When such a profession and action is undertaken, not only will the faith community hold that person accountable, but so can the civic opinion. Churches today are returning to public declarations with baptism in the following ways:

- Baptisms at outdoor venues such as rivers, parks, lakes, and even oceans;
- Baptisms at neighborhood or local events;
- Testimonials from those being baptized, live and/or recorded; and
- Video or audio recording of baptism and testimonials, then posting electronic video, pictures, and/or testimony via social media.

Step 2: Link Learners into a Small Group.[3] As we saw in chapters 3 and 4, small groups are some of the best venues for discipleship (making ongoing, active learners). While step 1 creates a personal and civil connection to Christ for the new learner, getting that learner quickly into a small discipleship group promotes his or her ongoing, active learning.

Many youthful and growing churches, such as St. Thomas' Church in Sheffield, England, actually require prospective members to participate in a small group.[4] Joining a small group creates a weekly, social link between new learners and a community of learners. This concept is not new to Anglicans, since John Wesley required weekly attendance in a small group (called "class" or "band" meetings) before he would allow an individual to attend the larger worship celebrations.[5] Think of what this would do today if we followed Wesley's practice and required small group participation before a person could attend weekend worship services.[6]

Requiring small group attendance of new Christians might be difficult for churches with historically lax membership requirements. But for newly planted churches, church restarts, and small congregations, it is often feasible and practical. At least churches must offer and encourage new Christians to participate in small groups where they create a give-and-take discussion environment that encourages learning.

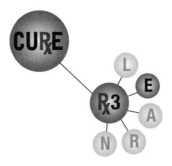

CURₓE E = EVERY SMALL GROUP BECOMES A
LEARNING GROUP

Don't Leave Out Any Groups

In chapter 3, we saw why in biblical times and today small groups are the best environment for discipleship to take place. In chapter 4, we saw how to get every small group involved in three areas of ministry: upward to God, inward to serve each other, and outward to serve non-churchgoers. Now we will see how to get small groups even more involved in learning.

It starts by counting all your existing small groups. In chapter 4, we did this by surveying all of the formal and informal small groups in your church, including boards, committees, Sunday schools, home fellowship groups, Bible studies, prayer groups, sport teams, worship teams, and other groups.[7] If you did not read chapter 4, go back and skim the section "CURₓE S: Survey Your Small Groups" to get an idea of how many small groups you already have. Here is the comprehensive definition we used in figure 4.1.

Figure 6.1: *A Comprehensive Definition of a Small Group*
Any regular gathering within a church's fellowship network, meeting more than one time a month with typically less than twenty attendees.[8]

If a different group of leaders counted your small groups in chapter 4, then obtain the list so you can help all the small groups

---

identified to become learning communities too. Once you have this list, it is time to grow every single small group into a learning environment.

Getting a small fellowship or task group focused on learning might, at the outset, seem challenging since most already have an agenda: a lead worship, exercise board responsibilities, organize an activity, lead a Bible study, host a Sunday school class, or something else. But most small groups can become learning environments simply by adding spiritual questions for discussion to their agendas.

Agenda Questions that Nurture Learners

John Wesley was noted for the use of required questions in small groups to create dialogue and spiritual learning. Wesley, who turned the tides of English spirituality, did so through a method of requiring these questions as agenda items. Let's look at some agenda questions that can stimulate spiritual discussion and learning.

Sermon-Based Agenda Questions. We saw in chapter 4 that one of the best ways to unite a congregation is for all segments of the church to study the same thing. Many churches utilize sermon-based questions in their small groups to create this. Often in this scenario, the preacher prepares a series of questions based on the previous week's sermon.[9] These questions encourage the small group participants to go deeper into the message and application to their local context. This sermon-based discussion strategy was the second "L" in chapter 4's "CURE Grow S.M.A.L.L.: Locate Your Focus in Small Groups." There we saw examples of churches that have created unity and learning by employing sermon-based questions.[10]

A caveat should be mentioned here. Many preachers seem to dislike the thought of having small groups dissect their sermon through such questions. This is a fear that must be overcome.

The importance of making learners in small groups trumps the preacher's insecurities. We all know that congregants talk about the sermon anyway. In this manner at least, the preacher has a chance to frame the questions and topics. Therefore, it is critical for preachers to overcome any reticence.

Lifestyle-Based Agenda Questions. The questions Wesley required were very poignant that make people squirm today no less than they squirmed back then. But such disquieting questions are needed today, especially when the media bombards us with ever more sexualized and sensationalized themes. The church must not shirk her responsibility to help people discuss and learn a biblical perspective on such issues.

Below are some of Wesley's questions.[11] They are given here to provide an introduction to the personal issues that Wesley thought should be addressed in discipleship venues.

- Have you the forgiveness of your sins?
- Have you peace with God, through our Lord Jesus Christ?
- Have you the witness of God's Spirit with your spirit that you are a child of God?
- Is the love of God shed abroad in your heart?
- Has no sin, inward or outward, dominion over you?
- Do you desire to be told of all your faults, and that plain and simple?
- Do you desire that every one of us should tell you from time to time whatsoever is in his heart concerning you?
- Consider! Do you desire we should tell you whatsoever we think, whatsoever we fear, whatsoever we hear, concerning you?
- Do you desire that in doing this we should come as close as possible, that we should cut to the quick, and search your heart to the bottom?

- Is it your desire and design to be on this and all other occasions entirely open, so as to speak everything that is in your heart, without exception, without disguise, and without reserve?

Some groups that have a close relationship might be able to use most of these questions immediately. Other groups with less intimacy may need to start with just one or two. But the key is to progress ever deeper into these questions.

Figure 6.2 gives a sample agenda that sets aside time for questions on spiritual matters. Figure 6.3 suggests questions that can foster learning during each of these agenda segments.

Figure 6.2: *Sample Agenda for Creating Learners with UP-IN-OUT Reflection*

Meeting Agenda

Call to order

IN Reflection, 10 minutes: Use questions and ideas from figure 6.3

OUT Reflection, 10 minutes: Use questions and ideas from figure 6.3

UP Reflection, 10 minutes: Use questions and ideas from figure 6.3

Reading and approval of the minutes

New business

Old business

Adjournment

Figure 6.3: *Questions and Ideas for Creating Learners with UP-IN-OUT Reflection*[12]

At each small group meeting, choose questions and ideas from each category to stimulate reflection. Cover all three of the UP-IN-OUT areas to maintain balance.

IN questions and ideas[13] 10 minutes minimum (Start with IN and OUT reflections to understand churchgoers and non-churchgoers' needs before taking your requests to God.)	Ideas
	• Divide into prayer triplets, and share your needs.
	• Pick a Scripture verse and tell what it means to you: Psalm 73:26; Proverbs 17:22; Matthew 6:30; Mark 14:38; Romans 15:4; Philippians 4:6.
	Questions to create reflection
	• How is God dealing with me lately?
	• What sins am I struggling with? (This is one of several "Wesley questions," which should be asked with discretion regarding attendees and venue.)
	• What secrets am I holding that I need to share among friends? (Another Wesley question.)
	• Do I insist on doing something about which my conscience is uneasy? (Another Wesley question.)
	• Is there anyone whom I fear, dislike, disown, criticize, hold resentment toward, or disregard? If so, what am I doing about it? (Another Wesley question.)

continued

Figure 6.3: *Questions and Ideas for Creating Learners with UP-IN-OUT Reflection* *continued*	
OUT **questions** **and ideas** 10 minutes minimum	Ideas • Divide up into prayer triplets, and share needs you have seen going unmet among non-churchgoers. • Pick a Scripture verse and tell what it means to you: Matthew 7:7–14; Luke 4:18–19; 1 Corinthians 1:3–5; 1 Timothy 6:12; James 1:26–27. • Go into your neighborhood and ask someone, "What can churches like ours do to meet needs in this community?" Questions to create reflection • What did I do last week to meet someone's need? • Am I consciously creating the impression that I am better than I really am? (Another Wesley question.) • What is a need of non-churchgoers of which I have recently become aware? • When did I last speak to someone else of my faith? (Another Wesley question.) • Does what I do as a Christian match what I say about being a Christian?
UP **questions** **and ideas** 10 minutes minimum	Ideas • Divide into prayer triplets and pray for one another's needs. • Pick a Scripture verse and tell what it means to you: Deuteronomy 31:6; Matthew 22:37–39; John 14:1–4; Romans 4:19–22; 1 Corinthians 1:3–5; Galatians 2:20; Ephesians 2:8; 1 Timothy 6:12; James 1:26–27. • Do a prayer walk around the immediate neighborhood. • Choose one of the Scriptures above and meditate on it, asking God to reveal its power to you. Questions to create reflection • What do I want to say to God about the pain in my life? • Did I give God a chance to speak to me each day this week? (Another Wesley question.) • When this week was life flowing out of me? • When this week was life flowing into me?[14] • Have I spent sufficient time with God and my family this week?

For More Information Read:
• Appendix 6.B: "Bible-Based Agenda Questions"

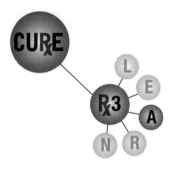

CU℞E A = AGREEMENT EMERGES FROM LEARNING

Outcomes of Spiritual Learning

One of the hallmarks of the early church was that Christians were growing in trust and unity. Luke said, "All the believers were united and shared everything. They would sell pieces of property and possessions and distribute the proceeds to everyone who needed them" (Acts 2:44–45 CEB). The verses below also underscore that trust and unity should be a trademark of Christians:[15]

- "I give you a new commandment: Love each other. Just as I have loved you, so you also must love each other. This is how everyone will know that you are my disciples, when you love each other" (John 13:34–35 CEB).
- "Now I encourage you, brothers and sisters, in the name of our Lord Jesus Christ: Agree with each other and don't be divided into rival groups. Instead, be restored with the same mind and the same purpose" (1 Cor. 1:10 CEB).
- "Finally, brothers and sisters, good-bye. Put things in order, respond to my encouragement, be in harmony with each other, and live in peace—and the God of love and peace will be with you" (2 Cor. 13:11 CEB).

A visible outcome of spiritual learning should be a heightened unity and agreement in a congregation. Sadly, this is often not the case. But if our churches begin to focus on making active, ongoing learners as the goal in lieu of inconsequential differences, then unity can result. Let me explain why.

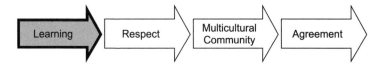

Learning Creates Respect

When different cultures, ethnicities, and traditions start to learn about one another, respect and tolerance usually grow.[16] So spending more of a church's time on making active, ongoing learners about one another and our differences can foster more respectful people.

However, I am not talking about tolerating open sin in a congregation (see Paul's harsh reprimand about this in 1 Cor. 5–6). Rather, I am talking about learning about other cultures, ethnicities, and religions to create open, honest, and helpful dialogue. This is the traditional meaning of tolerance, for according to Webster tolerance means "to recognize and respect [others' beliefs and practices] without sharing them," and "to bear or put up with [someone or something not especially liked]."[17] One author commenting on traditional tolerance said, "This attitude is basically what Paul expressed in 1 Corinthians 13:7, when he said that love 'endureth all things' (KJV)."[18]

Learning creates a respect for traditions, preferences, and customs without accepting or supporting sinful practices, ideas, or principles. Such respect allows an Anglo church to host a Hispanic worship service in its building once the Anglo church understands the background, history, and differences that a Hispanic congregation might prefer. As a result, the learning church can respect a different form of worship because it has studied its origin, rationale, and power.

Such respect is critical to growing an uncommon church. Our churches today are commonly monocultural enclaves, where biases and preconceived notions can inadvertently be nurtured.[19] Yet, the Scriptures on page 112 remind us that Christians are to be known by their unity and love. Thus, the place where questions and learning about cultural differences, practices, and customs should be fostered (with resultant unity) is the church.

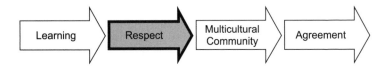

Respect Creates Multicultural Community

Once respect has been established, a church can begin to dialogue with other cultures and eventually partner with them in spiritual and kingdom growth. For instance, multiethnic churches have developed when people of different cultures connect and partner in the same church to advance God's kingdom. Researchers also know that biases are overcome and harmful stereotypes are reduced when people of different cultures fellowship with one another.[20] Before that fellowship emerges, respect sets the tone. In a world that is increasingly segmented, the church can and should be a place where understanding is created amid different cultures.

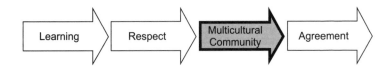

Multicultural Community Creates Agreement

When life is lived together (such as in a multicultural church),[21] people have to learn how to get along to run the church. Learning goes both ways between cultures as they partner to expand God's kingdom. A byproduct of this partnering is that stereotypes are further broken down and biases addressed.

Still, sometimes people think that learning will create walls and divisions. And when learning is one way (only from a leader to followers), then learning can become slanted, stifled, and divisive. But learning based on candid, honest, and two-way dialogue between teacher and pupil accelerates learning. Figure 6.3 gave suggestions for improving this two-way learning process. The result of such openness, candidness, and community dialogue is usually more unity, which is a sorely needed testimony in an increasingly factional world.

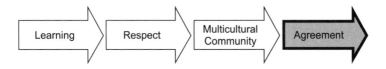

Agreement Results in an Uncommon Congregation

Churches today are commonly regarded as divisive and narrow-minded. But in Scriptures on page 112, we saw that Jesus had no such intention for his church. And so, to be an uncommon church today means to demonstrate respect, dialogue, and unity that gains the respect of the divided non-churchgoing world. And once this begins in our small groups, it can then expand throughout a congregation and into a community.

Instead of talking about our minor preferences and trivial differences, uncommon churches nurture knowledge seekers with a congregational focus on active, ongoing learners. The Bible reminds us, "An understanding heart seeks knowledge; but fools feed on folly," and "An understanding mind gains knowledge; the ear of the wise seeks knowledge" (Prov. 15:14; 18:15 CEB). Agreement amid diversity is a needed and welcomed outcome of the learning church.

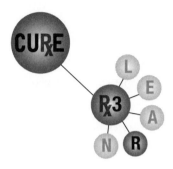

CU$_X$E R = REPRODUCTIVE LEARNERS PRODUCE MORE LEARNERS

Where Any Learner Can Become a Teacher

For learning to occur, a church must also have an open and clear route into leadership for new pupils. This begins with the open expectation that there is no role or position to which a pupil cannot aspire and one day attain. This means that a church has an attitude of advancement, where anyone can be used by God for his purposes. Lovett Weems in his book *Leadership in the Wesleyan Spirit* points out that it was this potential for leadership advancement that was a key to John Wesley's success.[22]

Reproductive Leadership—Every Teacher Mentors Someone

The key to creating an environment for unlimited advancement is to require that each leader be mentoring his or her replacement. This is sometimes challenging for churches where certain volunteers have held onto their jobs for many years and fear losing the status or responsibility they have attained. But creating a learning environment requires that all leaders become reproductive leaders, meaning that each leader is held accountable to be mentoring someone to take over for him- or herself.

The Mentor Cycle

Mentoring is sometimes easier if it is seen as a cycle with the following four principles. In figure 6.4, the process starts at the top and progresses clockwise. Each principle demonstrates a foundational attitude that must be developed between the mentor and mentee before the mentoring relationship can move further along the circle.

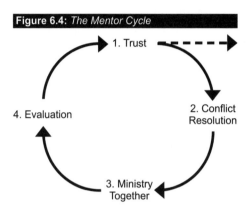

Figure 6.4: *The Mentor Cycle*

Trust. To begin, there must be a level of trust between the mentor and mentee. This means that both trust the personal traits of the other, including aptitude, Christlikeness, and honesty. Strengths and weaknesses of both mentor and mentee must be acknowledged as well. Trust is built on a sharing of parameters for time commitment and accessibility. Each party thus describes what they each want to see as outcomes. At this stage, you will also describe when and where each of the following three stages will take place (this is especially important for the often overlooked stage of evaluation).

Conflict Resolution. Because any relationship will yield conflict, the next level is to agree to resolve any conflict, discuss conflict resolution tools, and how you will handle conflict. Finally, discuss how seemingly unresolveable conflict will be mediated.

Ministry Together. This is where the actual ministry takes place. This includes open dialogue about progress, deficient areas (in both mentor and mentee), successes, and missteps.

Evaluation. In every mentorship cycle, evaluation must be a regular and ongoing part of the four-phase process. Here the mentor and mentee look back on the commitment documents that were drafted in the trust phase. The mentor and mentee decide if outcomes have been met and if it is time for the mentee to mentor as well. (The dotted line on figure 6.4 represents the mentee leaving the initial mentorship cycle and going out to mentor another.)

Figure 6.5 gives a suggested mentor and mentee statement of commitment and outcomes. Use this figure as a template to create your own. Remember, by utilizing such mentoring guidelines, the church becomes a network of learners where pupils are given the opportunity to grow into more responsibility and ministry.

Figure 6.5: *Mentor and Mentee Statement of Commitment and Outcomes*	
Fill in and agree on areas under each topic.	
MENTOR	*MENTEE*
1. Trust	
Personal characteristics:	*Personal characteristics:*
1. My strengths	1. My strengths
2. My weaknesses	2. My weaknesses
Commitment:	*Commitment:*
3. Time (weekly/monthly and mentorship duration):	3. Time (weekly/monthly and mentorship duration):
4. Openness:	4. Openness:
5. Outcomes (when you will know the mentorship is fulfilled):	5. Outcomes (when you will know the mentorship is fulfilled):
2. Conflict Resolution	
Under what circumstances will I do the following:	*Under what circumstances will I do the following:*
6. Compromise:	6. Compromise:
7. Acquiesce:	7. Acquiesce:
8. Mediate:	8. Mediate:
9. Terminate the relationship:	9. Terminate the relationship:
3. Ministry Together	
10. When:	10. When:
11. Where:	11. Where:

continued

Figure 6.5: *Mentor and Mentee Statement of Commitment and Outcomes* continued

4. Outcomes	
15. Outstanding: 16. Acceptable: 17. Not acceptable: 18. When will I know I am ready to mentor another?	15. Outstanding: 16. Acceptable: 17. Not acceptable: 18. When will I know I am ready to become a mentor?

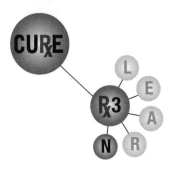

CURE N = NEEDS ARE MET THROUGH
LEARNING-BASED ACTION

Learning Is a Means to the End of Serving

The final element that creates a learning organization is an understanding that learning is not an end in itself. When organizations start to think that learning is the goal, then missteps such as figure 6.6 result.

Figure 6.6: *Mistakes That Arise When Learning Alone Is the Goal*

Problem	Source	Example
Unearned authority	When learning is the goal (and not making learners), then those with higher levels of learning are given more credence and authority. Churches that focus solely on learning create educational hierarchies, where people with greater education wield power regardless of suitability or spirituality.	Pastors and church leaders often laud their seminary degrees, seeming to infer that their seminary education makes them more knowledgeable about what will work in the local context than people actually from that local area. This can result in pastoral control issues.
Privilege	When learning becomes the goal, people often bestow privileges upon those with advanced learning that others do not enjoy. This creates further separation of teacher from learner (and can stifle the learner's growth).	Pastors and church leaders take privileges given to them by society and inadvertently create walls of separation and possibly resentment from pupils as well as neighbors.[23] *continued*

Figure 6.6: *Mistakes That Arise When Learning Alone Is the Goal continued*		
Problem	Source	Example
Code words	When learning is the goal, teachers often use code words (words not known by novices) to demonstrate the leader's advanced training. While there is nothing wrong with using terminology when warranted, some teachers use code words as a way of superiority and competition.	Understanding the Bible's Greek and Hebrew can throw light on what the writer was trying to say (as we saw in this chapter). But the use of too many code words can signify a leader wanting to demonstrate that he or she possesses knowledge that followers don't.

But what is the purpose of all this learning? Certainly it is to better understand our loving Father, but it is also something more. Let's look at what Jesus taught his disciples about an important aim of their learning.

Jesus Told Us to Serve Others with Our Knowledge

Jesus reminded his disciples, who were often struggling with vanity and self-importance, that greatness was defined by their level of and passion for serving others.

For example, in Matthew 23:1–12, Jesus illustrated how his followers should behave in contrast to the educated Pharisees, who used code words and privilege to receive unearned authority. Jesus warned,

> The legal experts and the Pharisees sit on Moses' seat. There-fore, you must take care to do everything they say. But don't do what they do. . . . They love to be greeted with honor in the markets and to be addressed as "Rabbi." But you shouldn't be called Rabbi, because you have one teacher, and all of you are brothers and sisters. . . . Don't be called teacher, because Christ is your one teacher. But the one who is greatest among you will be your servant. All who lift them-selves up will be brought low. But all who make themselves low will be lifted up. (vv. 2–3, 7–8, 10–12 CEB)

Serving others is the topic of chapters 1 and 2. These chapters came first in this cure for the common church for a reason: serving the needs of non-churchgoing people is a foundational aim of our learning. Our learning is not to receive privilege or authority, but, as Jesus reminded us, to "love the Lord your God with all your heart, with all your being, and with all your mind. This is the first and greatest commandment. And the second is like it: You must love your neighbor as you love yourself" (Matt. 22:37–39 CEB).

CONCLUSION

That's the next to the last cure! R3: for the common church is to grow L.E.A.R.N.ers with the following structure:

- **CURE L:** Link learners publicly with a community of learners.
- **CURE E:** Every small group becomes a learning group.
- **CURE A:** Agreement emerges from learning.
- **CURE R:** Reproductive learners produce more learners.
- **CURE N:** Needs are met through learning-based action.

QUESTIONS FOR GROUP AND PERSONAL REFLECTION

CURE L = LINK LEARNERS PUBLICLY WITH A COMMUNITY OF LEARNERS

Question 1: How was public testimony connected with your baptism, or was it connected to a recent baptism you observed? How were small groups connected with your baptism, or were they connected to a recent baptism you observed?

Begin this discussion by brainstorming two ideas that could connect baptism with a public declaration. Then brainstorm two ideas that could connect baptism with a small learning group.

Share your ideas with others. Which two ideas are most likely to be addressed? How will you endeavor to implement them?

CU℞E E = EVERY SMALL GROUP BECOMES A LEARNING GROUP

Question 2: What parts do spiritual reflection and spiritual questioning play in your small group life (committee work, board responsibilities, team work, Sunday schools, Bible studies, prayer meetings)?

- Take two of Wesley's questions from figure 6.3 and ask these questions of a small group in which you participate.
- Share the responses in general terms (be sure to share anonymously).
- What kind of mood did this create?
- What discussion resulted?
- Did learning take place?

Share your responses with one of your small groups. Then answer the question: What changes to your small group involvement could you make over the next sixty days to bring about more spiritual learning in such venues?

CU℞E A = AGREEMENT EMERGES FROM LEARNING

Question 3: In what areas does your church need unity? What questions need to be answered to bring about more unity?

Share your responses with one of your small groups. Are there areas of agreement? Disagreement? List two things you will do over the next thirty days to bring about greater unity in your church.

CURE R = REPRODUCTIVE LEARNERS PRODUCE MORE LEARNERS

Question 4: Are you mentoring someone to take over your job? If not, what are the obstacles to becoming a mentor? Fill out figure 6.5 for a potential mentee.

Discuss your answers with a group in which you have some degree of leadership. Ask them to give you ideas to overcome any obstacles to mentoring someone. List four benefits that could come from being in a healthy mentor and mentee relationship. Have them hold you accountable to create a mentor and mentee relationship.

CURE N = NEEDS ARE MET THROUGH LEARNING-BASED ACTION

Question 5: What have you been privileged to receive from your education or experience? Have you taken this honor for yourself, or have you used it to serve others? Tell how and in what ways.

Discuss your responses to the above question with others. Ask them to help you see blind spots when you honored yourself rather than served others. Ask them to hold you accountable to address your most obvious faults.

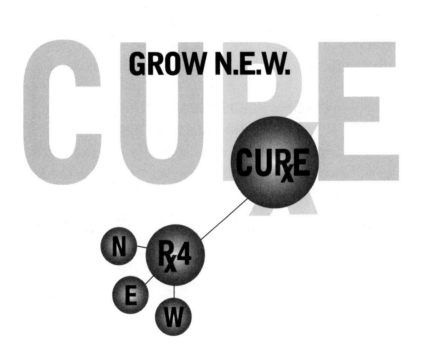

"Yours may be a COMMON CHURCH if . . ."
(SELF-SCORING—Check all that apply)

☐ Your church has experienced significant growth because of Christians moving into the area.

☐ Many of the young people who attend your church are relatives of existing church attendees.

☐ Many of your newcomers have transferred their attendance from another church.

☐ Your church is known as a church that is willing to try new ideas.

☐ Your church is known as the church that appreciates new styles of worship.

☐ Your church is primarily known for:

    ☐ Its social programs to help the needy.

    ☐ Its small group program.

    ☐ Its teaching and preaching.

    ☐ Its building and/or facility.

    ☐ Its good Sunday school program.

    ☐ Many of your newcomers have been previously connected with our denomination.

WHAT KIND OF NEW?

Most people who pick up this book are looking for a cure for the lack of enthusiasm and decline that has beset their congregations. As we saw in the Quick-Start Guide, it is common for churches to suffer from this.

So what is wrong with wanting to create a new church with vibrancy, life, and energy in hopes that it will grow and survive? Well, there is nothing wrong with this aim. But if the aim to become a new organization is your primary focus, you will never become uncommonly new. Let me explain why.

NEWNESS—4 TYPES

Church Newness

Often church leaders think that creating a new church organizational structure will revitalize their churches. Sometimes they do this by streamlining their hierarchy, simplifying their programs, firing or hiring staff, or merging a church with another congregation. The hope is that some organizational newness will foster a freshness that can revive the church. But if this is your strategy, you will fail at becoming a uncommon church.

Attempting to restructure the organization will not cultivate the supernatural community that God designed his church to be. New programs, staff, and structures will only survive until the next new thing emerges, and then the church will be antiquated (and common) again. Restructuring the church into something new, while laudable, cannot create a long-term uncommon church. This is because God desires that his church's newness emerge from people, not structures.

Newcomer Newness and Transfer Growth

Still other congregations hope that improving their hospitality and assimilation of newcomers will create a new church. Many helpful books can assist a church in better connecting newcomers to a congregation.[1]

But while connecting newcomers with a community of faith is an important task, it will not create the all-encompassing sense of newness that is needed to revive a common church. Newcomers certainly bring a sense of expectation, innovation, and camaraderie. In many churches, the newcomers are refugees from other churches, visiting a new church in search of something they are not getting at their previous congregation. There is a name for church growth that results from Christians church shopping: transfer growth.[2]

While transfer growth is important, since it helps ensure that Christians are getting plugged into a congregation, it does not create the kind of newness that an uncommon church needs. Donald McGavran said, "By transfer growth is meant the increase of certain congregations at the expense of others. . . . But transfer growth will never extend the church, for unavoidably many are lost along the way."[3]

For true newness to spread through a congregation, the supernatural newness that God intended is needed. This sense of newness arises from people in spiritual need being spiritually and physically transformed. Such newness pervades a congregation with a hope and passion that no other newness can match.

Churchgoer Newness

Many leaders want to see their church attendees changed. They are often tired of the wrangling, petty grudges, and poor attitudes that many churchgoers exhibit. They say to themselves, "If I could only change the people in the church and make them new, that would change the organization."

Changing people's attitudes is important. But churchgoer newness is not the vital type of newness that God intends to characterize the uncommon church. Another more never-ending newness is at the heart of God's purpose for his church. There is an eternal newness that springs forth when humans receive supernatural power to change their lives for the good and begin afresh.

Newness for Those in Spiritual Need

This is the true newness that will permeate the uncommon church. It is an expectation and invitation for people to be transformed physically and spiritually by a reunification with their loving heavenly Father (and among a community that embraces such newness). Figure 7.1 gives an overview of why and from where supernatural newness comes.

Figure 7.1: *An Overview of Newness for Those in Need*	
God cares about those in need.	• "I know that the LORD will take up the case of the poor and will do what is right for the needy" (Ps. 140:12 CEB). • "You have been a refuge for the poor, a refuge for the needy in distress" (Isa. 25:4 CEB).
God wants to bestow upon those in need a spiritual and physical newness.	• Jesus declared, "I came so that they could have life—indeed, so that they could live life to the fullest" (John 10:10 CEB). • "So then, if anyone is in Christ, that person is part of the new creation. The old things have gone away, and look, new things have arrived!" (2 Cor. 5:17 CEB).
Christians are to provide a fellowship that fosters and anticipates this newness.	• "True devotion, the kind that is pure and faultless before God the Father, is this: to care for orphans and widows in their difficulties and to keep the world from contaminating us" (James 1:27 CEB). • "Instead, when you give a banquet, invite the poor, crippled, lame, and blind. And you will be blessed because they can't repay you. Instead, you will be repaid when the just are resurrected" (Luke 14:13–14 CEB).

In the previous chapters, we saw that the term *missio Dei* describes God's quest to be reunited with his wayward offspring. Once this reunion is made, a real newness in personal lives emerges, a newness toward which the uncommon church will be orientated. Though growing O.U.T., S.M.A.L.L., and L.E.A.R.N.ers are part of the process, a church will not become uncommonly supernatural unless it welcomes and expects spiritual and physical transformation.

People today (but probably no more than in any other period) are in search of newness. They want to alleviate bad habits; overcome harmful enticements; curb destructive behavior; and be more loving, kind, and generous. But something deep inside of each of us seems to pull us back toward bad actions. The cure— the real, long-term cure—for uncommonness is a church where supernatural encounter and expectation is woven into the fabric of the congregation. And so, an uncommon church will exhibit many of the characteristics of figure 7.2.

Figure 7.2: *Church Patterns That Welcome Transformation*	
The uncommon church	• Expects miracles to happen. • Expects people to be changed in positive ways that no human effort could accomplish. • Expects people to show signs of growing in their dependence on God rather than dependence on humans. • Does not put its trust in programs, pastors, the past, or trends; but daily increases in their dependence on God's supernatural assistance to meet physical and spiritual needs.

WHY NEW IS NEEDED

Humans Are in a Pickle

As just noted, humans want to do the right thing, but we find ourselves constantly and repeatedly failing to do what we know is right. God knows we are prone to this (after all, he's a long-time observer of our behavior). And God has made a way for us to be changed. Figure 7.3 explains this fracture.

Figure 7.3: *Our Wrong Actions Fracture Our Fellowship with God*	
We have an inner pull that makes us do the wrong thing, even when we know better.	• "It wasn't so long ago that we ourselves were stupid and stubborn, dupes of sin, ordered every which way by our glands, going around with a chip on our shoulder, hated and hating back" (Titus 3:3 MSG).
These wrong actions separate us from our loving heavenly Father.	• "There's nothing wrong with God; the wrong is in you. Your wrongheaded lives caused the split between you and God. Your sins got between you so that he doesn't hear" (Isa. 59:1–2 MSG).
If we accept God's plan to have Christ bear our punishment, then God will restore our fellowship with him, help us change, and give us eternal life too!	• "But when God, our kind and loving Savior God, stepped in, he saved us from all that. It was all his doing; we had nothing to do with it. He gave us a good bath, and we came out of it new people, washed inside and out by the Holy Spirit. Our Savior Jesus poured out new life so generously. God's gift has restored our relationship with him and given us back our lives. And there's more life to come—an eternity of life! You can count on this" (Titus 3:4–7 MSG).

How Did God Create a Route Back?

Once humans see that we are prone to do what is bad for ourselves and that we are incapable of changing by ourselves, we then notice that God has created a route—a bridge—back to fellowship with him.

Figure 7.4: *God's Plan for a Route Back*	
Jesus took the punishment for our wrong actions so we could be restored to a close relationship with our loving heavenly Father.	• "But God put his love on the line for us by offering his Son in sacrificial death" (Rom. 5:8 MSG). • "Since we've compiled this long and sorry record as sinners (both us and them) and proved that we are utterly incapable of living the glorious lives God wills for us, God did it for us. Out of sheer generosity he put us in right standing with himself. A pure gift. He got us out of the mess we're in and restored us to where he always wanted us to be. And he did it by means of Jesus Christ" (Rom. 3:23–24 MSG).
Trusting in Jesus' actions will acquit us from the punishment due for our wrongdoings *and* give us a "whole and lasting life."	• "This is how much God loved the world: He gave his Son, his one and only Son. And this is why: so that no one need be destroyed; by believing in him, anyone can have a whole and lasting life. God didn't go to all the trouble of sending his Son merely to point an accusing finger, telling the world how bad it was. He came to help, to put the world right again. Anyone who trusts in him is acquitted" (John 3:16–17 MSG).
This route back is only available through Jesus Christ.	• "Jesus said, 'I am the Road, also the Truth, also the Life. No one gets to the Father apart from me'" (John 14:6 MSG).

How Do We Take That Route Back to God?

Now that we understand that God has created a route back to fellowship with himself, we begin to grasp that the all-powerful creator of the universe wants to have a personal friendship with each of us who will return. So what is involved in returning to him? The answer can be summed up in the statement of figure 7.5. Look at this figure, then examine three important concepts in it.

Figure 7.5: *How We Take the Route Back to God*[4]
Repentance must be combined with faith in order to bring about spiritual transformation.

Repentance. Repentance is a decision to "break with the past," which also carries the idea of turning and going in a new direction.[5] This is what it means when 1 John 1:9 says, "If we admit our sins—make a clean breast of them—he won't let us down; he'll be true to himself. He'll forgive our sins and purge us of all wrongdoing" (MSG).

People come to this stage when they realize they are dissatisfied with the ways their lives are going and know they need help beyond what humanity can provide. They may be frustrated that their lives are full of animosities, pride, biases, deceptions, conflicts, and a host of other maladies. And so they seek inner change.

The good news is that God wants that change for you too! He even promises to give you supernatural power to help you make those changes. It is this trust (or faith) in God's ability to help you that takes you to the next step.

Faith. Faith is a reliance and inner sense of knowing that God has the power to transform you.[6] The author of Hebrews offered a classic statement about faith: "It's impossible to please God apart from faith. And why? Because anyone who wants to approach God must *believe both that he exists and that he cares enough to respond* to those who seek him" (Heb. 11:6 MSG, emphasis added).

Author and lay theologian C. S. Lewis reminded us that faith also carries the idea of growing in unwavering faith when he wrote, "Faith . . . is the art of holding on to things your reason has once accepted, in spite of your changing moods."[7]

New People. Spiritual transformation in biblical terms means divine empowerment to reverse direction and go in the opposite way with your life.[8] Paul described it this way: "He gave us a good bath, and we came out of it new people, washed inside and out by the Holy Spirit. Our Savior Jesus poured out new life so generously. God's gift has restored our relationship with him and given us back our lives. And there's more life to come—an eternity of life! You can count on this" (Titus 3:5–7 MSG).

Therefore, when *repentance* (for our wrong doings) combines with *faith* (in Jesus Christ's sacrifice on our behalf), then *spiritual transformation* (into a new person) occurs.

This spiritual transformation into a new person has been called many things: conversion, salvation, being born again. Though these are important terms, they also have been mischaracterized. Unfortunately, to many people today, they do not bring to mind the original meaning of being transformed from our old way of living.

Today, *spiritual transformation* may be the best term to sum up what God is doing. When he creates a new person, our old desires for self-satisfaction and preferring ourselves over others will still be there, but spiritual transformation reminds us there is divine power to increasingly overcome these self-serving lures. And we experience emerging confidence and power as we see God daily helping us grow closer to him and as we participate in his mission. So spiritual transformation is a remarkable intersection of human will, Jesus' sacrifice, God's forgiveness, and a rekindled heavenward relationship. This is not a transformation that we can muster on our own. This is a change that goes deep to the core and purpose of the one who created us. It goes to the heart of our relationships with a heavenly Father who loves us and can help us.

The church is primarily a community that is collectively and constantly welcoming and experiencing this spiritual transformation where new people emerge. But the gloomy fact is that most commonly today, congregations are not experiencing this. This does several things to a church, including robbing it of its supernatural expectation and making it more familiar with churchgoers than non-churchgoers.

Thus, the how of growing N.E.W. is critical for nurturing an uncommon church. But before we get to that, let's look briefly at why spiritual transformation is at the pivot point of the uncommon church.

SPIRITUAL TRANSFORMATION IS A PIVOT POINT

What Is a Pivot Point?

Greek mathematician Archimedes emphasized the unlimited power of a lever when he stated, "Give me a place to stand, and I shall move the earth with a lever."[9] The key to the lever is the pivot or fulcrum point on which everything balances. Think of a teeter-totter with a balance point in the middle. Figure 7.6 illustrates such a teeter-totter with a triangle in the middle. The place where this triangle touches the teeter-totter board is the pivot or fulcrum point.

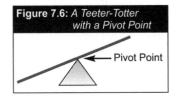

Figure 7.6: *A Teeter-Totter with a Pivot Point*

Pivot Point

Transformation as a Pivot Point

The pivot point is the place where balance can be created between the two sides of the teeter-totter. And the transformation of the person via faith and repentance is so critical that it is helpful to picture it as a fulcrum point that holds up and balances the methods of growing O.U.T. on one side and growing S.M.A.L.L. and L.E.A.R.N.ers on the other. Figure 7.7 illustrates this balance.

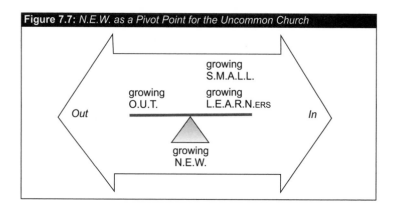
Figure 7.7: *N.E.W. as a Pivot Point for the Uncommon Church*

Spiritual Transformation as a Waypoint

Spiritual transformation is a pivot point because it is also at a critical waypoint between O.U.T., S.M.A.L.L., and L.E.A.R.N.ers. When a person is outside—not yet reunited in her or his relationship with God—and headed into a small environment of learning, somewhere along the way the person should encounter a transformative and pivotal experience with God.

Transformation is not optional for an uncommon church. Any church that focuses on growing O.U.T., S.M.A.L.L., or L.E.A.R.N.ers and neglects growing N.E.W. will not find balance in its efforts to fulfill God's ultimate aim. God's mission is to reunite and transform his wayward children, and no amount of good deeds through growing O.U.T. (no matter how helpful) will replace his yearning to intimately reconnect to his children.

Balance in the Uncommon Church

And so, the uncommon church does not have a lop-sided ministry toward O.U.T. on one hand or S.M.A.L.L. or L.E.A.R.N.ers on the other, but rather it balances all three on the foundational pivot point of N.E.W. In the next chapter, we will learn the three hows of N.E.W. But before we move on, go back to figure 7.7 to visualize that N.E.W. is not an optional prescription, but the pivot point upon which God intends the other prescriptions to be built and balanced. Without a church that embraces newness to balance the other cures, no holistic and uncommon church can ever emerge.

TAKE A LOOK

For More Information Read:
- Appendix 7.A: "Three Things That Are Not Newness but Can Lead to Newness"
- Appendix 7.B: "Why N.E.W. Creates Balance among the Four CUREs"

8 | HOW DOES A CHURCH GROW N.E.W.?

In this chapter, we will look at how an uncommon church fosters newness. In the previous chapter, we looked at why this newness is important, discovering that:

- God loves his offspring, wants to restore his relationship with them, and desires to meet their physical and spiritual needs.
- One of humanity's most widespread needs is for a physical and spiritual change (this has been described as conversion, being born again, being saved, spiritual and physical transformation, or emergence of new people).
- God has made it clear that only through Jesus Christ can such a complete transformation take place.
- Turning from our wrong actions (repentance), knowing that with Jesus' power we can change (faith), and then going in a new direction with God's help (spiritual and physical transformation) is God's desire for every person.

- God designed the church to explain this good news.
- God designed the church to welcome this transformation.
- Spiritual and physical transformation is the pivot point for the uncommon church (balancing the other three cures).

Let us look now at how an uncommon church fosters spiritual and physical transformation.

SITTIN' ON THE DOORSTEP WITH JERRY

"I knew how to survive in the streets," Jerry told me. "It's here among Christians that I was not at home." Jerry had been the manager of a local grocery until the store was purchased by a large chain, and Jerry's job was eliminated. Financial problems and a divorce soon sent Jerry from the church he had attended since he was a youth. "I grew up in that church," Jerry recalled. "But my ex-wife and kids go there, and I wanted to give them some space." And so began Jerry's church shopping that now was at an end.

As we sat on a doorstep on a gritty urban street Jerry, opened up about the spiritual journey that brought him there. "When I left that church," Jerry said, "I started attending Main Street Church a few blocks north. It was an old, established church, and I figured they would have ministries that could help me deal with my marital problems and get me a job too. It sure didn't happen." Jerry continued to tell of a church that seemed more concerned about his bad habits than his soul. "I always felt guilty around them. And they were pretty good about reminding me of my faults. I guess they had a reason for treating me that way. I was still doing some pretty bad things, and that really riled them up. I'm not even sure I was a Christian back then. I guess I needed to change, really change, like I'd never changed before. I was just trying to find people who would give me the time and the help to make it happen."

Jerry's next stop was Trinity Church. "At Trinity, they helped me find housing, got me a job interview, and even gave me a suit to wear to it. I'd say they helped up to a point."

"Up to what point?" I asked. "The point to where I needed to change more than just on the outside. I had a part-time job, an acceptable place to live, but I really needed a whole new start. I needed to understand my relationship with God. I needed to ask him to forgive me, and what he wanted me to do with my life. I needed to ask him to help me overcome the addictions that I couldn't overcome myself."

"Did you ask him?" I interjected.

"I asked them, the church leaders, but they said that was really between me and God. I remember the pastor saying, 'Jerry, you've got to decide for yourself what you believe about God. What I believe may not be what you need to believe.' I was more confused than ever," he said.

"So, I kept visiting churches because I needed to find people who were reconnecting to God and who could show me the way." Jerry visited church after church, until at last he found a Christian community that seemed balanced in its focus on helping him physically and spiritually.

"They told me they understood where I was coming from. They didn't rush me, but made me feel like I could be part of their fellowship as long as I continued to grow in my understanding. It really came together when they told me about a road to Jesus. A 'Roman Road' they called it. I became a new Jerry not long after. And people say they can see it too. But it didn't stop there; those people stuck with me. I had some setbacks, but a group of them kept helping me get my life back on course. I guess they traveled the road with me."

With that, Jerry disappeared up the steps into the front door of a fellowship that had become his new spiritual family. This community of Christians had helped him get back on his feet financially and spiritually. I looked up at the sign above the door and realized that the Salvation Army continues to provide a good example for the uncommon church, because it works in ways the common church misses or overlooks. As Jerry disappeared up the stairs, I whispered a prayer: "Lord, please make more churches like the Salvation Army, ready to stick with people like Jerry so they can become healthy physically and spiritually."

℞4 FOR THE COMMON CHURCH = GROW N.E.W.

With this final cure, as in all the cures in this book, the prescription spells out the name of the cure:

- **CU℞E N:** Nonjudgmental atmosphere.
- **CU℞E E:** Explore the newness people crave.
- **CU℞E W:** Walk the bridge to newness with them.

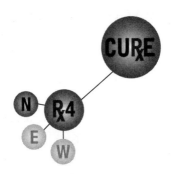

CU℞E N = NONJUDGEMENTAL ATMOSPHERE

Who Judges?

Everyone has a natural tendency to analyze the actions of others. And this tendency to judge can come from a good reason, such as a desire to help others overcome their faults and avoid pitfalls.

Whether it be a parent trying to guide a teenager away from temptation or a seasoned Christian trying to help a new churchgoer, judging actions and offering advice can be helpful.

But judging can be harmful too, especially if it is insensitive or comes from someone who does not have a relationship with the person being judged. Too often in our churches this is the case. We so desperately want to help new churchgoers that we pepper them with cursory advice from people they don't yet know. This was the problem that Jerry encountered at Main Street Church.

Does the Church Judge?

Religious people know that people's eternal destinies hang in the balance. Subsequently, religious people tend to create laws and regulations in hopes of keeping errant disciples from going astray. There is nothing wrong with the motivation, but when executed through an impersonal system of laws and rules, judging can actually drive people away. People need guidelines, but they also need those guidelines to be explained by a mentor whom they can trust and question.

During Jesus' time, a judgmental atmosphere had plagued Judaism for many years. Religious leaders created an impersonal system of rules that went far beyond the laws God had put forth in the Old Testament. Not surprisingly, Jesus had some of his harshest criticism for the judgmental attitude of the religious community, saying,

> Two people went up to the temple to pray. One was a Pharisee and the other a tax collector. The Pharisee stood and prayed about himself with these words, "God, I thank you that I'm not like everyone else—crooks, evildoers, adulterers—or even like this tax collector. I fast twice a

week. I give a tenth of everything I receive." But the tax collector stood at a distance. He wouldn't even lift his eyes to look toward heaven. Rather, he struck his chest and said, "God, show mercy to me, a sinner." I tell you, this person went down to his home justified rather than the Pharisee. All who lift themselves up will be brought low, and those who make themselves low will be lifted up. (Luke 18:10–14 CEB)

Why a Mentor Judges

As we saw in the beginning of this chapter, judging for the right reasons and in the right manner can be helpful. It can help people see that what they are doing is harmful to their physical and spiritual lives. Paul reminded Timothy that training, correction, and even censure have an important place in a Christian community: "Every scripture is inspired by God and is useful for teaching, for showing mistakes, for correcting, and for training character, so that the person who belongs to God can be equipped to do everything that is good" (2 Tim. 3:16–17).

Paul had a close, almost father-son relationship with Timothy. Paul was a mentor to Timothy, and Timothy would have understood Paul's admonition in light of Paul's model of close personal mentoring. Let's look at some ideas below for creating a nonjudgmental climate of mentorship in your church.

Fostering a Nonjudgmental Church Climate

Welcoming Spiritual Travelers. What should we call these people who seek to make sense out of their lives? They are often non-churchgoers, but this only describes their actions. Deep inside there is something more that is motivating them. They have an inner urge to seek stability and meaning in their lives.

Some authors call them "spiritual seekers," but many seekers may not yet know there is a spiritual component to their quests, so the term seems pejorative. Plus, they may only be seeking physical change. Historically, they have been called spiritual pilgrims, but in North America this conjures images of early American colonists.

Therefore, I shall describe them as spiritual travelers, for they are on a spiritual quest, seeking answers to their spiritual and physical needs from new friends and mentors. The key here is for the uncommon church to become aware of those who are on such quests and to be prepared to help them on their journey.

Allow Mentors to Show Mistakes. Too often it is the casual observer who feels beckoned to correct and censure such new churchgoing persons. Even when such advice is valid, it may fail to be received when it comes from a person without a personal and trusted relationship. And so, the uncommon church will have structures in place to help spiritual travelers quickly connect with a mentor who can then show mistakes to the seeker via a trusted, ongoing relationship.[1]

Figure 8.1 lists ideas that churches have used to connect newly transformed people to a mentor and discipleship group.

Figure 8.1: *Ideas for Establishing Mentor and Mentee Relationships*	
Spiritual traveler sponsors	These are mature Christians who agree to "sponsor" (mentor) new churchgoers. The sponsor is usually someone who has a similar lifestyle to the spiritual traveler in culture.[2]
Spiritual traveler small groups	These are small groups focused around the needs of new churchgoers. Led by two or more mature Christians, this group allows open questions about faith, history, and needs. I have used a model that includes a five-week traveler's class that continually restarts at the end of five weeks allowing non-churchgoers to jump in at any time.[3]
Spiritual traveler retreats	This involves a retreat weekend where new churchgoers are invited along with mature Christians to begin to foster either a mentor and mentee relationship or connect them to a small group. *continued*

Figure 8.1: *Ideas for Establishing Mentor and Mentee Relationships continued*	
Spiritual travelers invited to social clusters of three to five small groups	Mike Breen, the former rector of one of England's fastest growing churches, found that once a month combining three to five small groups into a social gathering often allowed spiritual travelers and potential mentors to get to know each other in a causal environment. They call these gatherings of three to five small groups clusters.[4] This clustering allows spiritual travelers to experience people from three to five small groups at a time and connect to the small discipleship group that is right for them.

But it is also important to remember that a good mentor is not afraid to delicately but decisively address character issues. A mentor must take his or her duty seriously. Accountability does not arise if the mentor is shy, timid, or intimidated. Remember 2 Timothy 3:16: "Every scripture is inspired by God and is useful for teaching, for showing mistakes, for correcting, and for training character" (CEB).

Allow Messy People in Your Church. The late Mike Yaconelli penned an insightful book with an unlikely title: *Messy Spirituality*.[5] In this book, he stressed that because the church is a place where hurting people come to be helped, we should expect the church to have some messiness, scruffiness, and untidiness in its atmosphere and in the behavior of its people.

I remember visiting an inner-city ministry center that was having a positive impact on its urban neighbors. I also noticed ashtrays outside the front doors and a disheveled group of men welcoming people into the auditorium. Later that day, I visited another church a few blocks away that was declining. I noticed their well-manicured lawn and well-kept church façade and how this contrasted with the gritty and growing urban ministry center just blocks away. The congregants of the tidy church wondered why urban residents who visited their pristine facility usually left in a few weeks. One member of the tidy church said to me, "I guess we expect cleaned-up Christians to visit us in search of help, but really in this area it is like Jesus said, 'send me the poor, the lame, the blind.'"

The verse wasn't quoted accurately by my friend, but the meaning was correct. In contrast to the religion of the Pharisees and Sadducees, Jesus was emphasizing that Christian community was to be a place where hurting people felt at ease and authentically welcomed, when he said, "When you host a lunch or dinner, don't invite your friends, your brothers and sisters, your relatives, or rich neighbors. If you do, they will invite you in return and that will be your reward. Instead, when you give a banquet, invite the poor, crippled, lame, and blind. And you will be blessed because they can't repay you. Instead, you will be repaid when the just are resurrected" (Luke 14:13 CEB).

For More Information Read:
• Appendix 8.A: "How Non-Churchgoing Spiritual Travelers Enter the Mentor and Mentee Cycle"

Therefore, the uncommon church is a place where people who are recently separated from their old ways of life may, for a while, still be hanging onto bad habits, foul language, destructive behaviors, and general spiritual untidiness. Certainly, these behaviors and attitudes should be addressed by mentors, but they also must be expected by all.

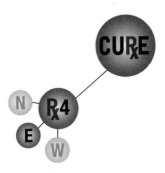

CU℞E E = EXPLORE THE NEWNESS PEOPLE CRAVE

Discovering What Newness a Person Needs

In chapter 2, we looked at how the uncommon church goes out to discover and meet the needs of people outside the church.[6] But meeting needs does not end in the first cure; it plays a key role in this cure too. In fact, identifying the needed change and then showing how Christ can meet that need is even more critical.[7] Here's why.

People usually sense a need for change immediately prior to the point of spiritual transformation. They feel that something in their lives is not right, and they want to change it. Usually they have tried to change it themselves but have been powerless to do so. It can be addictions, destructive habits, egoism, insensitivity, loneliness, and a host of other maladies. Before spiritual and physical transformation, there is usually a realization people have that they are not satisfied with their lives and they want to change. This can involve several areas, including the following.

Problems with Self-Image. This means people considering spiritual transformation are usually unhappy and dissatisfied with how they have come to be viewed by others. They may be profane (using sexualized and/or bigoted language), insensitive (to family and children), dishonest (compulsive liars), prejudiced, having low self-esteem, or self-loathing.

Problems with Uncontrolled Behavior. They might have habits, reactions, addictions, or compulsions they are unable to control. It can be addiction to sex, destructive behavior, substance abuse, and a host of other compulsions.

Problems with Relationships. These are interpersonal problems that arise from damaged or flawed relationships. People often feel they need supernatural intervention to restore such relationships. And the Bible is full of examples of God supernaturally bringing this about, including the remarkable story of how God reunited an outcast named Joseph with the brothers who tried to kill him (Gen. 37–50).

Problem with Spiritual Destiny. Most people also feel an acute sense of hopelessness or lostness about why they have been created and where their destinies lie. This problem usually occurs with the above problems too. This is the most common newness that people yearn for. People crave to understand why they were born, what their purposes are, and where their destinies lie.

To meet these yearnings for newness, God replies, "I know the plans I have in mind for you . . . plans for peace, not disaster, to give you a future filled with hope. When you call me and come and pray to me, I will listen to you. When you search for me, yes, search for me with all your heart, you will find me" (Jer. 29:11–13 CEB).

Crises and Need for Transformation

Researchers[8] have long understood that people usually seek change in their lives while going through crises.[9] Figure 8.2 shows how different crises create varying degrees of a need to change.[10] The more severe crises (listed toward the top of the left column) create more motivation to change. Therefore, to help people change, an uncommon congregation will seek to first understand what crises people are going through and then what change they need.[11]

The middle column of figure 8.2 offers questions they may be asking, and in the right column are suggestions for meeting their needs. This scale is not a definite list of need-based ministries, but rather a guide toward helping Christians find and meet the spiritual newness people crave.

Figure 8.2: Crises and Need-Meeting Ministries

Crisis that fosters a desire for change (most severe at the top)	Questions being asked	Need-meeting ministries
1. Death of a spouse	• Did they go to heaven? • What will I do now?	• Grief-recovery group or course • Course or study on refocusing life
2. Divorce	• How did my behavior contribute?	• Divorce recovery group or course
3. Marital separation	• Can I prevent divorce?	• Group or course on marriage
4. Jail term	• What will others say? • Who will help with my behavior?	• Inclusion route for ex-offenders • Addiction recovery groups
5. Family member death	(see number 1 above)	
6. Personal injury or illness	• How will I pay my bills? • Can God heal me? • Who will help me through this?	• Benevolence program • Parish-nurse program • Prayer or healing opportunities
7. Marriage	• Are we truly compatible? • What kind of social environment will keep my marriage strong?	• Newly married group or course • Marriage enrichment groups • Marital counseling ministry
8. Fired from work	• How can I find a new job? • How will I pay the bills? • Who will help me with new skills?	• Résumé writing course • Job-placement counseling • Benevolence program
9. Marital reconciliation	(see numbers 2 and 3 above)	
10. Retirement	• What does God have in store for me? • Does my life still matter? • What should I do with my time?	• Second-career programs that help retirees enter the ministry. • Mentoring programs comprised of seniors

continued

Crisis that fosters a desire for change (most severe at the top)	Questions being asked	Need-meeting ministries
11. Change in family member's health	• Why does God allow suffering? • How can I help a sufferer? • Is there a purpose in suffering?	• Group or course on problem of pain • Group or course on grief recovery
12. Pregnancy	• Who will help raise my child? • Is abortion ethical?	• Support for new mothers • Adoption options
13. Sex difficulties	• Am I unattractive to my spouse?	• Group or course on self-image
	(see numbers 2 and 3 above)	
14. Addition to family	(see number 12 above)	
15. Business readjustment	• Can I support my family? • How will I stretch my budget?	• Job skill training • Group or course on finances
16. Financial status change	(see number 15 above)	
17. Death of close friend	(see number 1 above)	
18. Number of marital arguments or changes	(see numbers 2 and 3 above)	
19. High mortgage loan	• How will I pay for this? • Is this good stewardship?	• Budget planning class • Financial seminar or course
20. Foreclosure of mortgage or loan	(see number 19 above)	
21. Change in work responsibilities	• How do I get along with a new boss? • How do I take on these new responsibilities?	• Mentoring by those with good business relationships • Course or study on ethical decision making
22. Son or daughter leaving home	• What will I do with my time? • How will my child do?	• Ministries for empty-nesters • Small groups for empty-nesters
23. Trouble with in-laws	(see numbers 2 and 3 above)	
24. Outstanding personal achievement	• Will this success change me? • What are my obligations to God? • What platform does this give me?	• Group or course on servant leadership • Christian ethics in business
25. Spouse starts work	• How will we raise our kids? • Will we still spend time together?	• Group or course on multiple income family management
	(see numbers 2 and 3 above)	

Figure 8.2: *Crises and Need-Meeting Ministries* continued

Such crises, which send the spiritual traveler seeking change, can overwhelm travelers and navigators unless both consider that God may have a purpose in the trouble. God often uses such difficulties to get our attention about the importance of renewing our relationships with him. Here is how Paul described it: "Distress that drives us to God does that. It turns us around. It gets us back in the way of salvation. We never regret that kind of pain. But those who let distress drive them away from God are full of regrets, end up on a deathbed of regrets" (2 Cor. 7:10 MSG).

Discovering the Needs of Others

If God intends spiritual reconnection to be a reaction to crises, then how do we help people in the midst of their own crisis? And how do we know exactly which crises they are experiencing? There are two natural, organic ways to help those in difficult times.

Be a Friend. Becoming a friend and traveling along with someone on his or her spiritual journey in the role of a companion is the first and most beneficial step. Though we may also become his or her mentor, guide, and navigator, this process begins with being a friend. Proverbs 17:17 reminds us that friends reflect God's love, stating "Friends love all the time" (CEB).

Ask. After a friendship has begun, at some point you just have to ask about the crisis a friend is going through. Sometimes these struggles are so personal or unsavory that people are reluctant to share them even with a friend. John Wesley saw this problem and suggested questions for the small group meetings that would draw out people's needs (see chapter 4). Figure 8.3 lists ideas for discussion starters among friends, some adapted from Wesley's questions.

> **Figure 8.3:** *Questions for Discovering the Needs of Spiritual Travelers[12]*
>
> These questions should be asked with discretion. Many are variations of the questions John Wesley suggested. Remember, do not be judgmental and do not use these questions verbatim; rather use them as idea generators:
>
> - Do you have peace with God?
> - How is God dealing with you lately?
> - How do you feel about God? How do you think God feels about you?
> - Is there some thought or behavior that has dominion over you?
> - Is there something in your life you wish to change, but have been powerless to do so?
> - What faults are you struggling with?
> - What secrets are you holding that you need to share among friends?
> - What things do you do about which your conscience feels uneasy?
> - What do you want to say to God about the pain in your life?
> - When is life flowing out of you?
> - When is life flowing into you?

Discovering the Needs for Newness

From the above discussion, it is clear that starting new ministries to meet the transformation needs of others is critical. To decide which need-meeting ministry in the right column of figure 8.2 you should launch, use the questions in figure 8.3 and the following three steps.

Conduct a Confidential Poll of New Churchgoers' Needs for Newness. This can be done discreetly by an online survey with a confidentiality feature. Ask the questions in figure 8.4 of people who have started attending your church in the last eighteen months.

> **Figure 8.4:** *Questions for Discovering New Churchgoers' Needs*
>
> These are confidential questions. Please be as candid and straightforward as possible.
>
> 1. When you started attending our church, what was it that made you want to attend church?
> 2. What expectations of our church did you have that we have not yet met?
> 3. With God's help, what do you want your life to look like two years from now?
> 4. If you could change your life, which change would you make first?

Match New Churchgoers' Needs to New Ministries. Go back to figure 2.8 in chapter 2. This figure shows you how to draft a list of ministries that can meet the needs of spiritual travelers.

Annually return to your survey of spiritual travelers and adjust your ministries accordingly (we will talk more about this later when we look at an annual checkup that revisits the four cures for the common church).

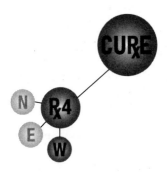

CUR̞E W = WALK THE BRIDGE TO
NEWNESS WITH THEM

The Bridge to the Eternal Cure

The final letter in the last cure is the most momentous. Here, two things are happening to people in spiritual and physical crises:

1. At this point, they realize that only God, the one who created them, can effectively and enduringly meet their needs.

2. They also feel that their relationships with God is estranged because they have ignored him for so long.

The good news is that though our misdeeds separate us from God, he has created a bridge back to a restored relationship with himself. There are four aspects to this restored friendship.

1. Our heavenly Father wants a close personal friendship with each of us.

- "He makes the creatures; the creatures don't make him. Starting from scratch, he made the entire human race and made the earth hospitable, with plenty of time and space for living so we could seek after God, and not just grope around in the dark but actually find him. He doesn't play hide-and-seek with us. He's not remote; he's near. We live and move in him, can't get away from him!" (Acts 17:25–27 MSG).

- "What's the price of a pet canary? Some loose change, right? And God cares what happens to it even more than you do. He pays even greater attention to you, down to the last detail—even numbering the hairs on your head!" (Matt. 10:29–30 MSG).

2. There is a rift in the relationship we each have with our loving heavenly Father.

- "There's nothing wrong with God; the wrong is in you. Your wrongheaded lives caused the split between you and God. Your sins got between you so that he doesn't hear" (Isa. 59:1–2 MSG).
- "If we claim that we're free of sin, we're only fooling ourselves. A claim like that is errant nonsense. On the other hand, if we admit our sins—make a clean breast of them—he won't let us down; he'll be true to himself. He'll forgive our sins and purge us of all wrongdoing" (1 John 1:8–9 MSG).

3. Our heavenly Father sent his only Son Jesus to provide the only bridge back.

- "Since we've compiled this long and sorry record as sinners (both us and them) and proved that we are utterly incapable of living the glorious lives God wills for us, God did it for us. Out of sheer generosity he put us in right standing with himself. A pure gift. He got us out of the mess we're in and restored us to where he always wanted us to be. And he did it by means of Jesus Christ" (Rom. 3:23–24 MSG).

- "This is how much God loved the world: He gave his Son, his one and only Son. And this is why: so that no one need be destroyed; by believing in him, anyone can have a whole and lasting life" (John 3:16 MSG).

- Jesus said, "I came so they can have real and eternal life, more and better life than they ever dreamed of" (John 10:10 MSG).

- "Jesus said, 'I am the Road, also the Truth, also the Life. No one gets to the Father apart from me'" (John 14:6–7 MSG).

4. We must accept the bridge God built and travel across it.

- "The jailer . . . asked, 'Sirs, what do I have to do to be saved, to really live?' They said, 'Put your entire trust in the Master Jesus. Then you'll live as you were meant to live'" (Acts 16:29–31 MSG).

- "That's salvation. With your whole being you embrace God setting things right, and then you say it, right out loud: 'God has set everything right between him and me!'" (Rom. 10:10 MSG).

- "Saving is all his idea, and all his work. All we do is trust him enough to let him do it. It's God's gift from start to finish! We don't play the major role. If we did, we'd probably go around bragging that we'd done the whole thing! No, we neither make nor save ourselves. God does both the making and saving. He creates each of us by Christ Jesus to join him in the work he does, the good work he has gotten ready for us to do, work we had better be doing" (Eph. 2:8–9 MSG).

- "A whole, healed, put-together life right now, with more and more of life on the way! . . . God's gift is real life, eternal life, delivered by Jesus, our Master" (Rom. 6:22–23 MSG).

The Importance of Walking the Bridge with Them

The uncommon church will foster an environment where helping others navigate this bridge is the norm. Therefore, the uncommon church walks this bridge with others, not retracing their own steps but walking alongside, helping, answering questions, and encouraging others as they cross a bridge between natural and supernatural living. A good reminder for us of the magnitude of the newness and that we represent God in it, can be found in 2 Corinthians 5:17–19: "What we see is that anyone united with the Messiah gets a fresh start, is created new. The old life is gone; a new life burgeons! Look at it! All this comes from the God who settled the relationship between us and him, and then called us to settle our relationships with each other. God put the world square with himself through the Messiah, giving the world a fresh start by offering forgiveness of sins. God has given us the task of telling everyone what he is doing. We're Christ's representatives" (MSG).

Everyone Must Learn at Least One of the Bridge Stories

As Christ's representatives, we need to tell others how God gave his Son to provide a bridge back to himself. I have found that in many growing churches, almost all congregants know how to explain the story of Jesus' bridge.

Thus, the last key toward helping others navigate the bridge back to a restored friendship with God is to have a congregation that can explain God's biblical bridge. Sometimes called the plan of salvation, these are simple memory devices that the majority of all attendees in the uncommon church must know if we are to fulfill Paul's admonition in 2 Corinthians 5:19: "God has given us the task of telling everyone what he is doing. We're Christ's representatives" (MSG). Here are three of the most common explanations of that bridge.

The Four Spiritual Laws[13]

God loves us and created each of us to know him personally (John 3:16; 17:3).

Humans are sinful and separated from God, so we cannot know him personally or experience his love (Rom. 3:23; 6:23).

Jesus Christ is God's only provision for human sin. Through him alone can we know God personally and experience his love (Rom. 5:8; 1 Cor. 15:3–6; John 14:6).

We must individually receive Jesus Christ as Savior and Lord; then we can know God personally and experience his love (John 1:12; Eph. 2:8–9; Rev. 3:20).

The Romans Road[14]

To aid in memorization, this explanation employs the metaphor of a Roman thoroughfare:

- Romans 3:23: "All have sinned and fall short of God's glory" (CEB). (Everyone needs salvation because we have all sinned.)
- Romans 6:23: "The wages that sin pays are death, but God's gift is eternal life in Christ Jesus our Lord" (CEB). (The price or consequence of sin is death.)
- Romans 5:8: "But God shows his love for us, because while we were still sinners Christ died for us" (CEB). (Jesus Christ died for our sins. He paid the price for our sins.)
- Romans 10:10: "Trusting with the heart leads to righteousness, and confessing with the mouth leads to salvation" (CEB).

(We openly declare that we receive salvation and eternal life through faith in Jesus Christ.)

- Romans 5:1: "Therefore, since we have been made righteous through his faithfulness combined with our faith, we have peace with God through our Lord Jesus Christ" (CEB). (Salvation through Jesus Christ brings us back into a relationship of peace with God.)

Steps to Peace with God[15]

This explanation uses phrases from John 3:16 as a memory tool:

- For God so loved the world: "I have loved you with an everlasting love" (Jer. 31:3).
- That he gave his one and only Son: "While we were sinners, Christ died for us" (Rom. 5:8).
- That whoever believes in him: "I am the LORD, the God of all mankind. Is anything too hard for me?" (Jer. 32:27).
- Shall not perish: "I give them eternal life, and they shall never perish" (John 10:28).
- But have eternal life: "Believe in the Lord Jesus, and you will be saved" (Acts 16:31).

So pick an explanation that works for you. But hold one another accountable to be able to explain at least one route, for 1 Peter 3:15–18 urges:

Be ready to speak up and tell anyone who asks why you're living the way you are, and always with the utmost courtesy. Keep a clear conscience before God so that when people throw mud at you, none of it will stick. They'll end up realizing that they're the ones who need a bath. It's better to suffer for doing good, if that's what God wants, than to be punished for doing bad. That's what Christ did definitively: suffered because of others' sins, the Righteous One for the unrighteous ones. He went through it all—was put to death and then made alive—to bring us to God. (MSG)

CONCLUSION

That's the cure! But R4 is the most vital, because it grows new lives, new hope, and new futures. The way the uncommon church fosters this is by growing N.E.W.:

- **CURE N:** Nonjudgmental atmosphere.
- **CURE E:** Explore the newness people crave.
- **CURE W:** Walk the bridge to newness with them.

Remember, there are four remedies in all, so don't just focus on this chapter. Keep in mind that this chapter helps people experience the newness that only God can bestow through his Son Jesus Christ.

QUESTIONS FOR GROUP AND PERSONAL REFLECTION

CURE N = NONJUDGMENTAL ATMOSPHERE

Question 1: Who has personally influenced your spiritual life for the better? Have you reciprocated by helping someone else in the same way?

Remember, creating a mentoring environment can offset a natural tendency of people to be judgmental. Though mentoring is a lost art in many churches, it still goes on informally in most congregations. Therefore, discover who are potential spiritual mentors and look into how you can organize their ministries by considering these idea starters:

- Who do most people in our church recognize as spiritual mentors?
- What can I (we) do to connect people struggling with their faith to one of these spiritual mentors?
- What would a job description for a spiritual mentor look like? List five things a spiritual mentor should do and three things he or she should not do.

Discuss with others what a ministry that connects spiritual travelers to spiritual mentors would look like. Put together a plan to implement this plan in the next sixty days.

CURE E = EXPLORE THE NEWNESS PEOPLE CRAVE

Question 2: Using figure 8.3, ask two non-churchgoing friends a few of these questions. What did you discover about their spiritual needs?

Begin by listing the spiritual needs you uncovered.

- Which were the most prevalent spiritual needs?
- Which of these could your church address?

Develop a plan for a new ministry your church could offer over the next two months that would meet one of these spiritual needs.

CURE W = WALK THE BRIDGE TO NEWNESS WITH THEM

Question 3: In one paragraph, write how you would explain the plan of salvation to a non-churchgoer. Do not use any helps to do this. For example, do not consult the various "plans of salvation" discussed elsewhere or in this chapter.

Once you have completed this,

- Consult the plans of salvation in this chapter and elsewhere. What parts of the plan were you missing or weak at addressing?
- Rewrite your personal plan after getting input from others and from the Bible.
- Memorize this plan and share it with a churchgoing friend. Are there parts still missing or underemphasized?
- Create an explanation of the plan of salvation that is biblically faithful and personalized to your experience. Commit this to memory and once a week, restate this plan in your devotional times. Ask God and others to show you ways to better communicate it.

90-MINUTE ANNUAL CHECKUP

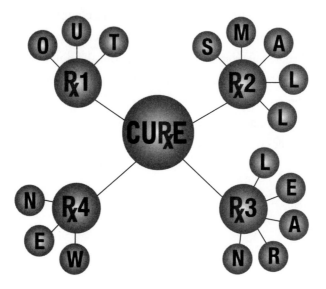

WHAT IS IT?

When you receive a prescription, the medical professional usually says, "Take all of your medication, until it is gone." The same is true with the cure for the common church. If a church stops taking its prescriptions before it has become healthy, the church will usually lapse back into ill health. Subsequently, I have found that a yearly evaluation and discussion of your road to health is critical to sustaining an uncommon church. And, this annual checkup need take only ninety minutes if it is focused around the results of a questionnaire filled out by participants prior to the meeting.

WHO LEADS IT?

In the Quick-Start Guide (pp. 11–17), church volunteers formed up to four strategy groups (T.E.A.M.s) and each agreed to investigate one cure. Annually, these T.E.A.M.s join together to sponsor a checkup meeting and invite all church attendees. The T.E.A.M. groups are ideal hosts because their responsibilities are:[1]

- Treatment: Each T.E.A.M. investigated one cure and suggested a treatment based on the prescriptions in this book.
- Educate: Each T.E.A.M. educated the congregation and the other T.E.A.M. groups about the church problems and the cures.
- Action Plan: Each T.E.A.M. drafted an action plan.
  - ▸ Sometimes a T.E.A.M. will have done the action plan itself.
  - ▸ Other times a T.E.A.M. may have delegated the action plan to an appropriate group within the church and then monitored their progress.
  - ▸ Each T.E.A.M.'s major focus was to generate a workable action plan from the cures in this book.
- Measure Progress:
  - ▸ Each T.E.A.M. created four-month goals. At the end of four months, all T.E.A.M.s came back together and shared their progress, holding one another accountable.
  - ▸ Together the T.E.A.M.s
    - ○ Administered a checkup survey at least thirty days before the annual checkup.
    - ○ Tabulated the results prior to the annual checkup.
    - ○ Hosted a 90-minute annual checkup, as an annual, church-wide reporting and listening session.

THE CHECKUP SURVEY

Prior to the 90-minute annual checkup, the T.E.A.M.s will administer the survey found in figure 9.1 and tabulate the results. Instructions for tabulating the results are contained in the section following the questionnaire.

Figure 9.1: *Checkup Survey*

(Note: This is an anonymous survey)

Questions for Our Church Attendees
(Poll one month prior to annual checkup)

1. Yes ___ No ___ Do you attend our church one or more times a month?
2. Yes ___ No ___ Are you regularly involved (one or more a times month) in any of the following groups that are sponsored by our church:
   - Sunday school classes
   - Leadership committees
   - Classes of any type (Bible-studies, topical classes, 12-step programs, etc.)
   - Home fellowship groups
   - Any kind of church team (ministry teams, worship teams, athletic-orientated teams, set-up teams, etc.)
   - Prayer groups
3. Has our church helped you learn more about God over the last year? (choose one response)
   - ☐ Much more   ☐ Somewhat less
   - ☐ Somewhat more   ☐ Much less
   - ☐ About the same
4. How long have you been a Christian? _____ years/months
5. How long have you attended this church? _____ years/months

For People Who Do Not Attend Our Church
(business leaders, city leaders, town or school board members, leaders of other churches, principals of schools, town employees, long-term community residents, etc.)

A. In your opinion, how is our church viewed by the community in comparison to last year? (choose one response)
   - ☐ Much more favorably   ☐ Somewhat less favorably
   - ☐ Somewhat more favorably   ☐ Much less favorably
   - ☐ About the same
B. If you wish, please explain why: _____
   _____
   _____
   _____

CONDUCTING THE 90-MINUTE ANNUAL CHECKUP

Add It to Another Meeting

The 90-minute annual checkup can take place in conjunction with another all-church gathering. In fact, I have found that it

---

works better when churches add this to a regularly scheduled event (as long as an extra ninety minutes can be set aside). This is because churches on their way back to health are often weighed down with church duties.[2] If you try to make the 90-minute annual checkup an extra meeting, it will usually be less effective and have fewer attendees than if you simply add it to another meeting.

T.E.A.M. Tasks at the Annual Checkup

Pre-Meeting Survey. The four T.E.A.M.s administer the survey at least one month before the 90-minute annual checkup.

Questions 1–5:

- are given to church attendees;[3]
- are administered via hard copy or electronic means;[4]
- are given to those in an agreed-upon age range (usually sixteen and older); and
- are given during two consecutive weekend church services (no more than ten minutes should be required to conduct the survey, and people who filled out the survey the first week are asked not to fill it out again).

Questions A–B:

- are given to community leaders, such as local officials, school principals and teachers, businesspeople, opinion makers, and residents involved in community service;
- are usually given via electronic means; and
- are requested to be returned at least two weeks before the 90-minute annual checkup meeting.

Tasks of T.E.A.M. 1 / CURE 1. This group analyzes the results from questions A and B. These questions are measuring the degree of positive impact the church is having among those outside of the church. This group is measuring changes in community appreciation for the church's ministry, and they conduct it in the following manner:[5]

- Questions A and B are given to community leaders who do not attend your church (though they may attend church elsewhere).
- T.E.A.M. 1 adds the number of responses for each opinion category.
- T.E.A.M. 1 compares the results to the previous years and tracks changes, looking for improvement or deterioration.[6]
- T.E.A.M. 1 asks, "Why did these changes take place?"

Tasks of T.E.A.M. 2 / CURE 2. This group calculates the year-to-year changes in the percentage of regular attendees that are involved in small groups. In chapters 3 and 4, we saw that it is in small group environments where accountability, spiritual growth, and leadership development happens. Thus, T.E.A.M. 2 conducts its analysis in the following manner:

- T.E.A.M. 2 compares the results of question 2 (number of people who attend a small group) with the results from question 1 (the number of regular church attendees).
- T.E.A.M. 2 computes the percentage of regular church attendees who also attend small groups.
- T.E.A.M. 2 compares the results to the previous years, and tracks changes, looking for improvement or deterioration.[7]
- T.E.A.M. 2 asks, "Why did these changes take place?"

Tasks of T.E.A.M. 3 / CURE 3. This group tabulates the year-to-year changes in the number of people who say that over the last year the church has helped them learn more about God. Their analysis is conducted in the following manner:

- T.E.A.M. 3 adds the number of responses for each opinion category of question 3.
- T.E.A.M. 3 compares the results to the previous years, and tracks changes, looking for improvement (movement toward more learning).[8]
- T.E.A.M. 3 asks, "Why did these changes take place?"

Tasks of T.E.A.M. 4 / CURE 4. This group calculates one of the most important measurements of all. This is how many people are experiencing a new relationship with God as part of their faith journey with your church. This group compares questions 4 and 5 to see who became a Christian while attending your church (conversion growth) or if they were a Christian before they started attending your church (transfer growth).[9] T.E.A.M. 4 conducts its analysis in the following manner:

- T.E.A.M. 4 compares each response of how many years or months the person has been a Christian (question 4) with how many years or months the person has attended the church (question 5). If the conversion total is equal to or less than the attendance total, then they have probably experienced new life while attending your congregation.
- T.E.A.M. 4 adds the number of survey respondents who have become Christians while attending your church.
- T.E.A.M. 4 tracks this number and looks for increases from year to year.[10]
- T.E.A.M. 4 asks, "Why did these changes take place?"

The Tasks of All T.E.A.M.s—Keep the Meeting Focused on Listening

The secret to successful meetings in today's hectic world is to not try to cover everything, but to give people thinking points and feedback that can help them mull these ideas over between meetings. I've found that a ninety-minute meeting, when the moderator holds everyone to a strict schedule, can be an annual checkup time that people will look forward to attending. Figure 9.2 gives a suggested schedule.

Figure 9.2: *Suggested Meeting Schedule*	
First sixty minutes:	1. Each of the four T.E.A.M.s share the results from their part of the survey in no more than fifteen minutes per team. 2. No questions are allowed until all four T.E.A.M.s have presented their results (this is because the cures are interrelated, and attendees must have a full understanding of the cures' regimen).
Next thirty minutes: (While this may go longer than thirty minutes, it is best to aim for brevity.)	1. Ask for input from attendees. 2. T.E.A.M. secretaries record input and discussion. 3. T.E.A.M.s refrain from making plans during this time. This is a listening time. It will be after the meeting that the T.E.A.M.s will meet to adjust their plans.
After the meeting:	1. T.E.A.M.s meet no later than thirty days after the checkup to consider the input they received and adjust their plans. 2. T.E.A.M.s continue to meet at least once every four months until the problem is addressed. 3. The T.E.A.M.s administer the survey again every twelve months.

For More Information Read:
- Appendix 9.A: "Sample Schedule for an Annual Checkup Retreat"
- Appendix 9.B: "The Biblical Basis of the Survey Questions"
- Appendix 9.C: "Health Is a Circular Process That Is Never Finished"

Yes, that's it. The regimen for health and growth begins with four cures that address the problems at the heart of weak, divided, and dying churches. Then strategy T.E.A.M.s divide up to work on each cure while charting progress and keeping the health regimen on course. Finally, a church-wide yearly checkup measures progress.

Then your church can join other uncommonly healthy and growing churches. And your answers to the questions below will be much different than when you started this book.

"Yes, yours may be an UNCOMMON CHURCH if . . ."

(SELF-SCORING—Check all that apply)

☐ You are seeing spiritual and physical conversions happening in people's lives.

☐ Your church is more unified than last year.

☐ Your church is increasing in its help to people outside of the church who are in need.

☐ More and more church attendees are involved in leadership and serving others.

☐ Newcomers regularly get involved in your church.

☐ Attendees say they regularly learn something new about God at your church.

☐ More and more church attendees are getting involved in small groups (committees, fellowship groups, Bible studies, prayer groups, etc.).

☐ People in the community are increasingly appreciative of the things you are doing for the community.

☐ Your church is creating cultural harmony and understanding in the community.

☐ Your church is more diverse than ever.

☐ Going to church is a highlight of your week.

☐ God is working miracles in your church!

NOTES

Additional resources and complete notes are available online at www.wesleyan.org/wph/cureresources.

Quick-Start Guide

1–5. See online notes.

6. Duke University, *National Congregations Study*, accessed October 16, 2011, http://www.soc.duke.edu/natcong/index.html.

7. See online notes.

8. George Hunsberger, "Introduction," in *The Church Between Gospel & Culture: The Emerging Mission in North America*, ed. George R. Hunsberger and Craig Van Gelder (Grand Rapids, Mich.: Eerdmans, 1996), xiii.

9–10. See online notes.

Chapter 1

1. See online notes.

2. Donald A. McGavran, *Understanding Church Growth* (Grand Rapids, Mich.: Eerdmans, 1970), 295–313.

3. The experience trap was first discussed in David L. Dotlich and Peter C. Cairo, *Unnatural Leadership: Going Against Intuition and Experience to Develop Ten New Leadership Instincts* (San Francisco: Jossey-Bass, 2002), 75–78.

4. Roy H. Lubit, "The Long-Term Organizational Impact of Destructively Narcissistic Managers," *The Academy of Management Executive* 16, no. 1 (February 2002): 127–138.

5–7. See online notes.

Chapter 2

1–2. See online notes.

3. "Demographic," Dictionary.com, accessed August 15, 2012, http://dictionary.reference.com/browse/demographic.

4–6. See online notes.

7. The phrase "talk alike, behave alike, and can tell who is in their group and who is not," is expanded by Paul Hiebert in more detail as a matrix of behaviors, ideas, and products (*Cultural Anthropology* [Grand Rapids, Mich.: Baker, 1976], 25).

8–16. See online notes.

17. Barry A. Kosmin and Ariela Keysar, *The American Religious Identification Survey (ARIS) 2008* (Hartford, Conn.: Program on Public Values, 2009) and Duke University, *National Congregations Study*, accessed August 4, 2011, http://www.soc.duke.edu/natcong/index.html.

18–29. See online notes.

Chapter 3

1–3. See online notes.

4. Barry A. Kosmin and Ariela Keysar, *The American Religious Identification Survey (ARIS) 2008* (Hartford, Conn.: Program on Public Values, 2009); and "What's the Size of US Churches?" accessed August 4, 2011, http://hirr.hartsem.edu/research/fastfacts/fast_facts.html#sizecong.

5–8. See online notes.

9. LeRoy Eims, *The Lost Art of Disciple Making* (Grand Rapids, Mich.: Zondervan, 1978), 45–46.

10. See online notes.

11. Eddie Gibbs, *I Believe in Church Growth* (Grand Rapids, Mich.: Eerdmans, 1981), 236.

12. See online notes.

13. Tim Albin interviewed by Tim Stafford, "Finding God in Small Groups," *Christianity Today*, August 2003, 42.

14. See online notes.

15. Thom Rainer, *Surprising Insights from the Unchurched and Proven Ways to Reach Them* (Grand Rapids, Mich.: Zondervan, 2001), 120.

16. Ray C. Stedman, *Body Life: The Book That Inspired a Return to the Church's Real Meaning and Mission* (Grand Rapids, Mich.: Discovery House, 1972). See especially chapter 10, "Keeping the Body Healthy" where Stedman suggests that small groups are the needed glue to create unity and spiritual growth in a church.

17. John Wimber and Sam Thompson, *Kinships: Home Fellowship Groups,* audio cassettes (Vineyard Ministries International, 1986).

18. See online notes.

19. Lyle E. Schaller, *Effective Church Planning* (Nashville: Abingdon, 1981), 17–63.

20. Kent Hunter, *Heart-to-Heart Groups* (Corunna, Ind.: Church Growth Center, 1990).

21. C. Peter Wagner, *Your Church Can Grow* (Glendale, Calif.: G/L Publications, 1976), 107–108.

22. Eddie Gibbs, *Body Building Exercise for the Local Church* (London: Falcon, 1979), 55.

23. Larry Osborne, *Sticky Church* (Grand Rapids, Mich.: Zondervan, 2008).

24. Nelson Searcy and Kerrick Thomas, *Activate: An Entirely New Approach to Small Groups* (Ventura, Calif.: Regal, 2008).

25. Andy Stanley and Bill Willits, *Creating Community: Five Keys to Building Small Group Culture* (New York: Multnomah, 2004).

26. Rainer, *Surprising Insights*, 120.

27. Osborne, *Sticky Church*, 28–29.

28–34. See online notes.

Chapter 4

1–2. See online notes. For more on what it means to make disciples and the central place disciple-making has in the church's mission, see Matthew 28:19–20, and the discussion of this passage in chapter 5 of this book.

3. Bob Whitesel, "How to Missionalize Your Small Groups," in *Organix: Signs of Leadership in a Changing Church* (Nashville: Abingdon, 2011). Note that small groups will often grow larger than twenty attendees, but when they do, closeness and intimacy break down.

4. Lois Y. Barrett, et. al., *Treasures in Clay Jars: Patterns in Missional Faithfulness* (Grand Rapids, Mich.: Eerdmans, 2004), xii–xiv.

5. This icon is a modification of the triangle as described by Mike Breen and Walt Kallestad, *The Passionate Church: The Art of Life-Changing Discipleship* (Colorado Springs: Cook, 2005).

6. Bob Whitesel, *Growth by Accident, Death by Planning: How Not to Kill a Growing Congregation* (Nashville: Abingdon, 2004), 142–143; following Eddie Gibbs, "Groups and Growth," in *I Believe in Church Growth* (Grand Rapids, Mich.: Eerdmans, 1981), 240–255.

7–12. See online notes.

13. Charles Arn, *Heartbeat! How to Turn Passion into Ministry in Your Church* (Camarillo, Calif.: Xulon, 2010); Thom Rainer, *Surprising Insights from the Unchurched and Proven Ways to Reach Them* (Grand Rapids, Mich.: Zondervan, 2001), 120.

14. See online notes.

15. Rainer, *Surprising Insights*, 120.

16. Larry Osborne, "Sermon-Based Small Groups," *Sticky Church* (Grand Rapids, Mich.: Zondervan, 2008), 73–158.

17. See online notes.

Chapter 5

1–2. See online notes.

3. Hudson Taylor quoted by Stan Toler, *Stan Toler's Practical Guide to Solo Ministry* (Indianapolis: Wesleyan Publishing House, 2008), 136; C. T. Studd quoted by David L. Marshall, *To Timbuktu and Beyond: A Missionary Memoir* (New York: Thomas Nelson, 2010), 87; William Carey quoted by A. Scott Moreau, Gary B. McGee, and Gary R. Corwin, *Introducing World Missions: A Biblical, Historical, and Practical Survey* (Grand Rapids, Mich.: Baker Academic, 2004), 201; C. S. Lewis, *The Complete C. S. Lewis* (New York: HarperOne, 2002), 96.

4. Daniel B. Wallace, *The Basics of New Testament Syntax: An Intermediate Greek Grammar Basics* (Grand Rapids, Mich.: Zondervan, 2000), 274–275. A good way to think of this is that the participles (go,

baptizing, teaching) tell how making disciples is done. Thus, to the question, "How do you make disciples?" one could answer, by going (means) and baptizing (manner) and teaching (manner).

5. See online notes.

6. Wallace, *The Basis of New Testament Syntax*, 280. "*A greater emphasis is placed on the action of the main verb than on the participle.* That is, the participle is something of a prerequisite before the action of the main verb can occur" (italics Wallace). In other words, the "going," "baptizing," and "teaching" are prerequisites that must occur before the action of the main verb ("making disciples") can take place.

7. *A Greek-English Lexicon of the New Testament and Other Early Literature*, trans. William F. Arndt, and F. Wilbur Gingrich (Chicago: University of Chicago Press, 1957), 486–487.

8. Donald McGavran, *Effective Evangelism: A Theological Mandate* (Phillipsburg, N.J.: Presbyterian & Reformed, 1988), 17.

9. Eddie Gibbs, *Body Building Exercises for the Local Church* (London: Falcon, 1979), 74.

10. James F. Engel, *Contemporary Christian Communications: Its Theory and Practice* (New York: Thomas Nelson, 1979), 66.

11. See online notes.

Chapter 6

1–4. See online notes.

5. Joel Comiskey, "History of the Cell Movement," accessed November 1, 2011, http://www.joelcomiskeygroup.com/articles/tutorials/cellHistory-1.html.

6–7. See online notes.

8. Bob Whitesel, "How to Missionalize Your Small Groups," in *Organix: Signs of Leadership in a Changing Church* (Nashville: Abingdon, 2011).

9. See Larry Osborne, "Sermon-Based Small Groups," *Sticky Church* (Grand Rapids, Mich.: Zondervan, 2008), 73–158.

10. See online notes.

11. John Wesley, *The Works of John Wesley*, vol. 9 of *The Methodist Societies: History, Nature, and Design*, ed. Rupert E. Davies (Nashville: Abingdon, 1989), 77–78.

12. These questions are adapted and codified from several sources: D. Michael Henderson, *A Model for Making Disciples: John Wesley's Class Meetings* (Springfield, Mo.: Evangel, 1997), 118–119; Comiskey, "Wesley's Small Group Organization"; extracted with permission from Comiskey, "History of the Cell Movement."

13. Wesley, *Works*, 77–78.

14. This question and the one before it were described by Dr. Elaine Heath, "A Contemplative Vision for Christian Outreach" (presentation, The Academy for Evangelism in Theological Education, Chicago, June 16, 2011).

15. See online notes.

16. "Cross-Racial Understanding and Reduction of Racial Prejudice," Sothern Poverty Law Center, accessed June 14, 2011, http://www.tolerance.org/tdsi/sites/tolerance.org.tdsi/files/assets/general/ Cross-Racial_Understaning_and_Reduction_of_Racial_Prejudice.pdf.

17. "Tolerate," *Webster's New World Dictionary and Thesaurus* (Hoboken, N.J.: Wiley, 2002), 644.

18. Josh McDowell and Bob Hostetler, *The New Tolerance: How a Cultural Movement Threatens to Destroy You, Your Faith, and Your Children* (Carol Stream, Ill.: Tyndale, 1998), 16.

19. See online notes.

20. Melanie Killen and Clark McKown, "How Integrative Approaches to Intergroup Attitudes Advance the Field," in *Journal of Applied Developmental Psychology* (Philadelphia: Elsevier, 2005), 612–622. "These comprehensive educational studies conclude that racially integrated student body is necessary to obtain cross-racial understanding, which may lead to a reduction of harmful stereotypes and bias" from "Cross-Racial Understanding and Reduction of Racial Prejudice."

21. See online notes.

22. Lovett H. Weems, Jr. *Leadership in the Wesleyan Spirit* (Nashville: Abingdon, 1999), 59–70.

23. See online notes.

Chapter 7

1. Charles Arn, *Heartbeat! How to Turn Passion into Ministry in Your Church* (Camarillo, Calif.: Xulon, 2010); Gary L. McIntosh, *Beyond the First Visit: The Complete Guide to Connecting Guests to Your Church* (Grand Rapids, Mich.: Baker, 2006); Nelson Sercy with Jennifer Henson, *Fusion: Turning First-Time Guests into Fully-Engaged Members of Your Church* (Ventura, Calif.: Regal, 2008).

2. See online notes.

3. Donald A. McGavran, *Understanding Church Growth* (Grand Rapids, Mich.: Eerdmans, 1970), 72.

4. This statement is adapted with updated terminology from Richard Peace's terms in "Conflicting Understandings of Christian Conversion: A Missiological Challenge," *International Bulletin of Missionary Research*, vol. 28, no. 1, 8.

5. *Metanoia* (the Greek word for *repentance*), *A Greek-English Lexicon of the New Testament and Other Early Literature*, trans. William F. Arndt and F. Wilbur Gingrich (Chicago: University of Chicago Press, 1957), 513–514; see also Peace, "Conflicting Understandings."

6. *Pistis* (the Greek word for *faith*), *Greek-English Lexicon*, 668–670.

7. C. S. Lewis, *Mere Christianity* (San Francisco: HarperCollins, 2001), 140.

8. *Epistrophe* (the Greek word for *spiritual transformation* or *conversion*), *Greek-English Lexicon*, 301; see also Peace, "Conflicting Understandings."

9. E. J. Dijksterhuis, *Archimedes*, trans. C. Dikshoorn (Princeton, N.J.: Princeton University Press, 1987), 15.

Chapter 8

1–2. See online notes.

3. Bob Whitesel and Kent R. Hunter, *A House Divided: Bridging the Generation Gaps in Your Church* (Nashville: Abingdon, 2000), 181–184.

4. Mike Breen, conversation with author, Sheffield, England, June 10, 2009.

5. Mike Yaconelli, *Messy Spirituality* (Grand Rapids, Mich.: Zondervan, 2002).

6–7. See online notes.

8. This adaption of the Holmes and Rahe Readjustment Scale with the explanation of how varying crises affect a craving for spiritual transformation is based on Flavil Yeakley's PhD research. Flavil Yeakley, "Persuasion in Religious Conversion" (PhD dissertation, University of Illinois, 1976).

9–11. See online notes.

12. Compare D. Michael Henderson, *A Model for Making Disciples: John Wesley's Class Meetings* (Springfield, Mo.: Evangel, 1997), 118–119; and Joel Comiskey, "Wesley's Small Group Organization," extracted with permission from "History of the Cell Movement," accessed August 2, 2011, http://www.joelcomiskeygroup.com/articles/tutorials/cellHistory-1.

13. The "Four Spiritual Laws" was originally conceived by Campus Crusade founder Bill Bright (http://campuscrusade.com/fourlawseng.htm) but the original version seemed to build on people's more self-centered desire for attaining God's plan for their lives. While this is certainly valid, an alternative version is quoted here (compare http://www.4laws.com/laws/englishkgp) because it better emphasizes the *missio Dei* (God's desire to be reunited with his wayward offspring).

14. See online notes.

15. "Steps to Peace with God" was developed by the Billy Graham organization. It supports this presentation with an extensive web presence at http://peacewithgod.jesus.net.

90-Minute Annual Checkup

1–10. See online notes.